New Chairs

New Chairs

Design, Technology, and Materials

Mel Byars

Research by Cinzia Anguissola d'Altoé

Laurence King Publishing

LAURENCE KING

Published in 2006 by Laurence King Publishing Ltd
71 Great Russell Street
London WC1B 3BP
United Kingdom
Tel: + 44 20 7430 8850
Fax: + 44 20 7430 8880
e-mail: enquiries@laurenceking.co.uk
www.laurenceking.co.uk

A catalogue record for this book is available
from the British Library

ISBN-13: 978 1 85669 413 1
ISBN-10: 1 85669 413 5

Design concept by Struktur Design
Layout by Mel Byars

Printed in Singapore

Frontispiece: Sturdy Straws Chair by Tal Gur

Contents

Introduction: A World of Chairs

Twirl Lounge Chair:
Ronen Kadushin/Golmat

Pare Chaise Longue:
Anon Pairot/Planet 2001

Corallo Armchair:
Humberto Campana and
Fernando Campana/Edra

Paper Stacking Side Chair:
Raul Barbieri with
Anna Giuffrida/Plank

Carbon Side Chair:
Bertjan Pot and
Marcel Wanders/Moooi

The 67 chairs or suites here have been culled from those designed within the past few years. The number 67 has no significance—it is merely the largest number of examples that could be properly addressed in a book of this size.

The selection illustrates the wide range of advanced and traditional materials and production methods that are being employed today by imaginative designers and manufacturers.

While the uses and range of furniture types—particularly chairs—have remained more or less the same through the centuries, production demands today are rather different from in the past. In the process of realizing utilitarian objects, contemporary designers and manufacturers must satisfy a number of different criteria, such as production and shipping costs, the use of available or specially built machinery, safe disposal, reusage, and market demands.

It is no longer possible to know how a chair has been made simply by looking at a single attractive photograph of it in a decoration or design publication. Nor is it possible to know how the materials were employed and what the designers' and manufacturers' goals were. For example, the foam of Ronen Kadushin's springy Twirl Lounge Chair was not cut, as might be expected, with a hot wire, and he communicated with the manufacturer in an unusual manner.

Kadushin reveals the thinking behind his conception and describes the production process in his own words (pp. 100–01), as do most other designers here. Their comments—provided specially for this book—are intelligent, insightful, and, in some cases, endearing.

It should be obvious that the chairs here do not represent all of the issues and problems today facing those who create chairs as well as other furniture types. A mere 67 examples cannot hope to do this. However, a large number and a wide range of solutions pertinent to today are addressed through the more than 400 drawings and photographs of maquettes, machinery, deconstructions, configurations, and usage.

By now, design has lost much of its national identity. This is due to designers' awareness of what their counterparts are doing in other countries. Their expressions are individual but on the whole are realized in a somewhat narrow global language. There are exceptions, such as the Pare Chaise Longue by young Thai designer Anon Pairot (pp. 122–23). It is hand-built in rattan, native to Thailand, and was inspired by a traditional boat indigenous to the country.

The designers whose work is included here are active in a variety of countries: Brazil, Canada, the Czech Republic, Denmark, France, Germany, Iceland, India, Israel, Lebanon, the Netherlands, Poland, Sweden, Switzerland, the UK, the US, and, of course, Italy, which remains the home of high design. A number are émigrés: from Germany, Iran, and Japan, for instance. Design is an increasingly international phenomenon, with designers based in one country designing chairs that are then produced by companies in distant countries—this is now a norm.

Examples—both prototypes and multiple-production models—commonly express or use:
° Easy reconfiguration and customization by end users
° Ecological concerns
° Computer-numeric-controlled and laser-cutting machinery
° Inspiration from origami and nature
° Special machinery created for individual production
° Low-tech manufacture with high-tech materials
° High-tech manufacture with high-tech materials
° Complex materials never before employed in the furniture industry
° Solutions to diminish various costs.

Naturally, anyone looking at the chairs for the first time will respond emotionally to the aesthetics before any other aspect. Nonetheless, an intelligent discussion of any example will necessarily extend beyond personal opinion on form and color.

Should there be fewer prototypes and more mass-produced examples in the book? This was a difficult decision to make, because prototypes are often more interesting, innovative, and intelligent than designs and solutions that manufacturers adopt for the marketplace. Yet a number of Italian manufacturers continue to have the courage, taste, and money to support imaginative work. Companies that show this commitment include Edra (pp. 36–37) and Plank (pp. 20–21 and 44–45).

Often prototypes reveal the absence of the kind of knowledge, practical collaboration, patience, and funding that a sophisticated manufacturer can provide to realize a chair for production. Even so, no professional designer makes a prototype as an end-all exercise, unless it is art furniture, and there are few examples of that here (pp. 28–29, 104–05, and 132–33). Otherwise, all designers wish to have their work produced as multiples. Quantity is at the heart of industrial design and the driving force behind the profession's existence.

Yet due to the small number of superior manufacturers and the large number of talented designers working today, many designers have established their own production and marketing facilities. They include Tom Dixon (pp. 58–59) and Marcel Wanders (pp. 130–31).

Possible surprises in the book are the age of one of the designers (pp. 60–61) and the purpose of one of the chairs (pp. 62–63).

Collaborating with me once again, Cinzia Anguissola d'Altoé helped with the discovery of entries and the gathering of some materials.

The designers and manufacturers generously provided the technical information and all the images. They also arranged for reproduction permission from photographers, for which the publisher and I are grateful.

—Mel Byars

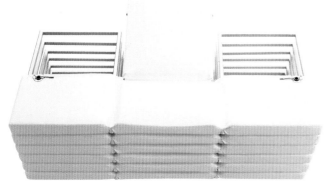

1

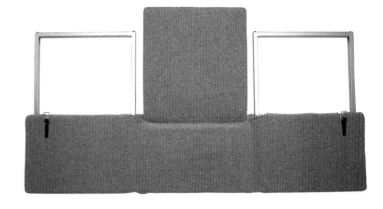

2

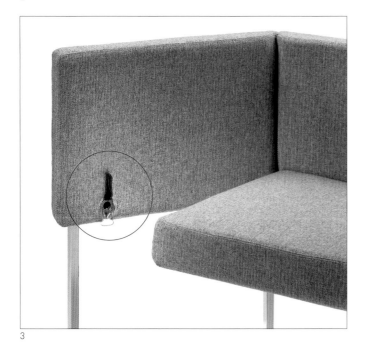

3

4

1. Six stacked examples occupy little space.

2. A single example is shown splayed.

3. The seat is folded upward and the arms inward. Metal hooks on the front sides of the seat are guided into the lower, inside area of the arms where an unobtrusive rotating / coupling device holds the seat firmly in place.

4. A fully and simply assembled armchair is shown with one of the choices of upholstery—leather.

Cubica Armchair

Designer	"Tito" Juan Bautista Agnoli (Italian-Peruvian, b. 1931)
Manufacturer	Zanotta S.p.A., Nova Milanese (MI), Italy
Date of design	2002
Materials	Painted or chromium-plated steel, polyurethane foam, fabric or leather upholstery
Size (mm/in.)	Flat: 1510/59⅜₆ long, 800/31½ high; assembled: 600/23⅝ wide, 720/28⅜ high, 530/20⅞ deep

Agnoli trained as a painter under Mario Sironi before completing his studies at the Politecnico in Milan. The Italian-Peruvian designer is now active in Como.

He prefers to work on the premises of his manufacturing clients so that he can collaborate directly with the administrators in the offices and the technicians on the floor of the plants.

Agnoli and Zanotta, like all designers and manufacturers, wish to achieve wide international sales. However, shipping costs, particularly for pieces of furniture that occupy large volumes, can be expensive. Thus, a collapsible padded chair

Photos: Marino Ramazzotti (p. 11; p. 10, bottom right); Adriano Brusaferri (others)

that occupies a small volume and can be assembled after its arrival at a store is highly desirable.

Unfortunately, much of the so-called knock-down furniture being produced today is not upholstered for comfort, has the appearance of being cheap, and lacks a level of high style for which the Italians, for example, have become known.

Agnoli's aesthetically sophisticated design—the Cubica Armchair—solves the problem so well that, were you to see it on display in a furniture showroom, you would be unlikely to suspect its completely flat knock-

down feature. The designer claims to have called on the principles of origami in creating it.

Concerning ease of assembly and aesthetics, Agnoli says: "The armchair volume flattens out thanks to a simple rotational and coupling mechanism.... The outcome... becomes pure shape."

He adds this insight into the solution: the configuration not only features "a new flexible and compact way of storing the product but also [provides] a new way of conceiving the production process—from molding to cover application... [then to] packing and shipping operations."

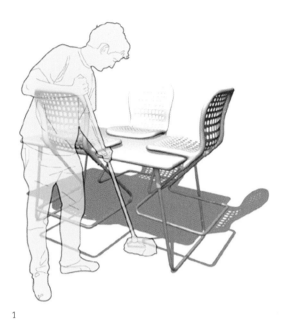

1

3

2

1–2. A group of Nic Chairs can be hung on the edge of a table to facilitate floor cleaning beneath.

3. The prototype for this chair, which was ultimately to be produced in a plastic material, was made using steel tubing and a welded pierced-metal sheet.

Nic Side Chair

Designer	Werner Aisslinger (German, b. 1964)
Manufacturer	Magis, Motta di Livenza (TV), Italy
Date of design	2003
Materials	Seat: 87.5% polypropylene, 12.5% fiberglass; connectors for leg attachment: 50% polyamide, 50% fiberglass for the outer bush and 100% polyamide for the inner bush; leg frame: 22 mm/⅞ in. dia. ASFORM 420 steel tubing (with a 2 mm/¹⁄₁₆ in. wall)—chromium-plated and bent with arc-welded pins
Size (mm/in.)	514/20¼ wide, 825/32½ high, 530/20⅞ deep, 480/18¹⁵⁄₁₆ seat height

Aisslinger studied under Hans Roericht at the Hochschule der Künste in Berlin before working in the studios of Ron Arad and Jasper Morrison in England and Andreas Branzi and Michele De Lucchi in Italy. He set up his own studio in Berlin 11 years ago.

Any designer might envy Aisslinger the commission for the Nic Chair owing to the advantages offered by the manufacturer: advanced technology, high-tech facilities, and potentially high sales. Not least, Aisslinger had the opportunity to collaborate with Eugenio Perazza, Magis's passionate, vivacious founder.

The designer conceived the Nic Chair with the underlying belief that innovative design is, or should be, driven
by technology. Air-molding is the primary technology
employed in the chair's production—a process pioneered
by Magis for high-design products, particularly seating.
Magis was in the vanguard in developing the furniture-
making process of blowing air into a tubular-plastic structure (a chair leg) and, thus, providing a high degree of
strength not found in solid tubular-plastic structures.

Concerning the method for attaching the seat to the
frame, Aisslinger has confessed: "Chairs don't need to

look like this, and, at least theoretically, it is entirely wrong
to cantilever a seat in this way… because it maximizes
the stress on the connection between the seat and frame."
As a result, a special seat-to-leg plastic unit had to be
developed. "But it is an elegant solution to chair design,"
Aisslinger says. "And, since the 1920s, designers have
wanted chairs where the seat seems to be suspended
freely in space on two legs."

Aisslinger also chose the configuration because this
type of structure permits a springiness which affords more
comfort than if the structure were rigid.

Testing and production follow >

BACK IMPACT TEST

S, Mises
SNEG, (fraction = -1.0)
(Ave. Crit.: 95%)

```
+2.154e+007
+2.034e+007
+1.915e+007
+1.795e+007
+1.675e+007
+1.556e+007
+1.436e+007
+1.316e+007
+1.197e+007
+1.077e+007
+9.573e+006
+8.376e+006
+7.180e+006
+5.983e+006
+4.786e+006
+3.590e+006
+2.393e+006
+1.197e+006
+0.000e+000
```

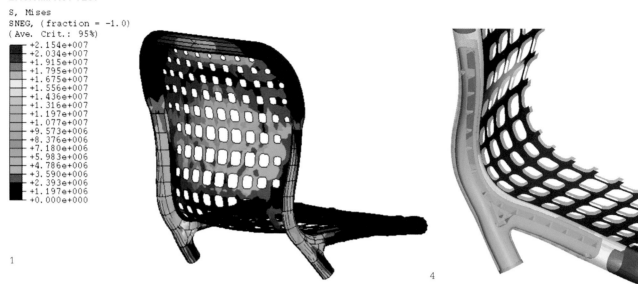

1

4

SEAT IMPACT TEST

S, Mises
SNEG, (fraction = -1.0)
(Ave. Crit.: 95%)

```
+5.366e+007
+5.068e+007
+4.770e+007
+4.472e+007
+4.173e+007
+3.875e+007
+3.577e+007
+3.279e+007
+2.981e+007
+2.683e+007
+2.385e+007
+2.087e+007
+1.789e+007
+1.491e+007
+1.192e+007
+8.943e+006
+5.962e+006
+2.981e+006
+0.000e+000
```

2

5

Pressure - Time Series (MPI2.0)
Time = 10.86[s]

[MPa]

```
30.00

29.98

29.96

29.94

29.93
```

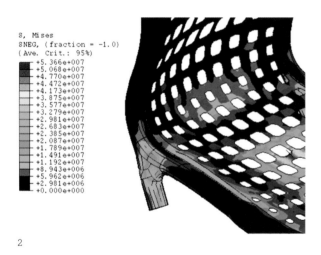

3

1–4. Stress tests were conducted on the frame and the seating unit to determine possible changes to be made to the plastic formula and thicknesses and even to the shape itself.

5. A casting of the seat, shown from the topside, has a flat surface at the edges. The material is 87.5% polypropylene and 12.5% fiberglass. The tubular air-blown section of the seat that provides strength follows the circumference at the backside and bottom side (not shown).

6. The die that forms the back face of the seat.

7. The back face of the die, shown again, with the seat/leg connector elements inserted into the edges of the die (see the red circle and image 4). The connector is made of 50% polyamide and 50% fiberglass for the outer bush and 100% polyamide for the inner bush.

8. The seat/leg connectors are molded in one die, separate from the seat unit. They are made of polyamide and polyamide/ fiberglass to provide extra strength to hold the tubular-steel legs in place and to avoid splitting.

9–11. A bending machine forms the leg frames precisely. The material is tubular ASFORM 420 stainless steel (22 mm/ ⅞ in. dia. with a 2 mm/¹⁄₁₆ in. wall) and is chromium- plated.

Photos: Gianfranco Pauletto (tube machine); Luca Scotti (tool); Andrea Evangelista (other production)

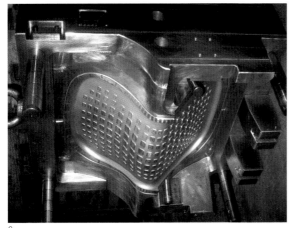

6

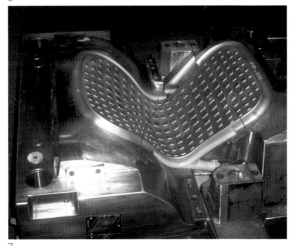

7

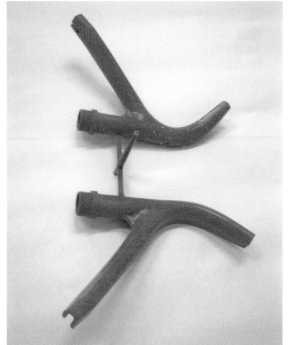

8

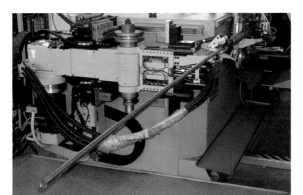

9

10

11

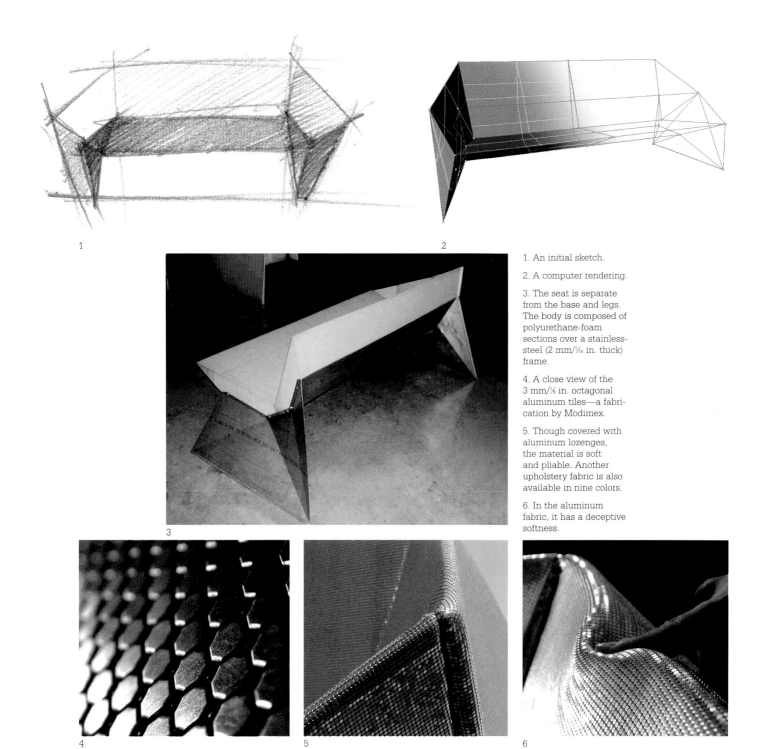

1. An initial sketch.

2. A computer rendering.

3. The seat is separate from the base and legs. The body is composed of polyurethane-foam sections over a stainless-steel (2 mm/¹⁄₁₆ in. thick) frame.

4. A close view of the 3 mm/⅛ in. octagonal aluminum tiles—a fabrication by Modimex.

5. Though covered with aluminum lozenges, the material is soft and pliable. Another upholstery fabric is also available in nine colors.

6. In the aluminum fabric, it has a deceptive softness.

Low Res Easy Chair

Designer	Dodo Arslan (Italian, b. 1970)
Manufacturer	spHaus S.r.l., Seregno (MI), Italy
Date of design	2003
Materials	Stainless-steel sheet, polyurethane foam, aluminum-lozenge or fabric upholstery
Size (mm/in.)	1000/39⅜ wide, 800/31½ high, 900/35⅜ deep

Arslan began the seating project using a skeletal frame. As he puts, it is "like a Vespa that has a chassis instead of a classical motorbike's frame and, [following] the cheapest way of doing a small production, employs polyurethane foam blocks." He suggests that its polygonal volumes "speak" an architectural language.

The next stage of development was inspired by the interlocking metallic facets of Paco Rabanne dresses—Arslan had seen these in Milan, which is where his studio is located. Subsequently, he found a micromosaic material composed of octagonal aluminum plates,

produced by Modimex, which reminded him of Rabanne's frocks. The Modimex fabric has also been used recently by some well-known fashion designers as well as by Swatch.

Arslan likes the material because its surprising softness contrasts with the chair's rigid volumes, which include approximately 24 polygonal planes. The few folds in the stainless-steel sheeting for the frame impart extreme strength.

The wide version is shown here, but a narrower one is also available.

1. The frame—steel tubing—is bent, precision-welded, painted, and screwed to the table top. The top is laminated plywood. The casters are polyamide.

2. The swivel cap is attached to the underside of the seat.

3. The seat—a beech plywood shell—features a lockable gas spring for height adjustment. The hook on the underside of the table can hold a student's bag(s) and frees up floor space.

4. A gathering of finished units and the machinery for their production.

5. Permutations of the units are almost infinite —to face the teacher, a wall display, a computer monitor, or anything else.

6. Student interaction and convenience are fostered by the easy mobility of the units.

The dimensions and structure satisfy the final Draft of European Educational Furniture Standards (prEN 1729 Parts 1 and 2).

1

2

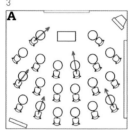

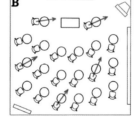

3

4

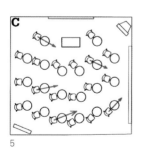

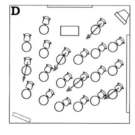

5

6

Orbital WorkStation

Designers	Shin Azumi (Japanese, b. 1965) and Tomoko Nakajima Azumi (Japanese, b. 1966)
Manufacturer	Ercol/Keen Group Ltd., Bucks., UK
Date of design	2003
Materials	Frame: precision-welded DIN 2391 steel tubing; lockable gas spring for chair-height adjustment: Stab-O-Block 75.5 stroke 150 N, manufactured by Stabilus; seat: beech plywood; table top: 15 mm/⅝ in. thick laminated birch plywood
Size (mm/in.)	1100/43⁵⁄₁₆ from the front of the table top to the rear of the chair, 680/26¾ wide

Shin Azumi initially trained as an industrial designer and Tomoko Azumi as an architect and worked for firms and studios in Japan. Subsequently, they attended the Royal College of Art in London. Soon after, in 1995, they set up their own studio, remaining in London.

In the beginning, they produced much of their furniture and other items themselves. Now, however, their work is being produced by a number of firms, including Isokon, for which they restyled the famous Penguin Donkey bookcases of 1936 and 1963.

They claim that the "entertaining aspects" of their

work stem from their time working as a director and art director with the Vital Theatre dance company at the 1993 Edinburgh Festival.

According to the Azumis, they "have been expanding their design territories from objects to space." An example is their Orbital WorkStation, one of the three winning entries (among 60 entrants) in the Furniture of the Future competition organized by the Design Council and the Department for Education and Skills in the UK. The competition was part of the Design Council's Kit for Purpose initiative aimed at making classrooms into more

nurturing places in 21st-century education.

The Azumis' chair/desk offers flexibility in a classroom setting, where the more traditional rows of seat/desk units, permanently attached to the floor, do not. The unit's name—Orbital—is derived from the ability it gives the student user to "orbit," or to rotate, the seat around the table.

Because students vary in body height (1.3 to 1.9 m/ 4 ft. 3 in. to 6 ft. 3 in. at eight years of age and older), the seat height is adjustable. And the entire unit can easily and silently be moved into various configurations.

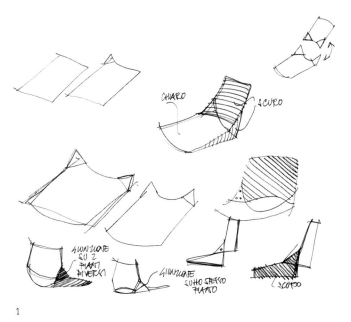

1

2

3

1. The original ideas differ appreciably from the final solution arrived at by the manufacturer's technicians.

2. Early miniaturized paper and metal experiments.

3. The ultimate solution for fusing the two identical sections of the shell.

4. A straight-leg side chair version and, not shown, one with arms are available.

5. The adjustable-height version with casters and a mono-material shell with a seat pad.

6. A version with each facet in a different color.

7. The caster version with arms.

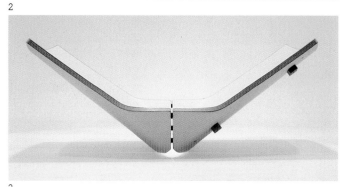

4

5

6

7

Paper Stacking Side Chair and Swivel Armchair

Designers	Raul Barbieri (Italian, b. 1946) with Anna Giuffrida (Italian)
Manufacturer	Plank Collezioni S.r.l., Ora (BZ), Italy
Date of design	2002
Materials	Frame: chromium-plated tubing; seat and back: molded plywood, veneered in various materials or laminated in various colors and textures
Size (mm/in.)	Varies according to model

Barbieri, who attended the Politecnico in Milan, got his first professional experience in the Olivetti design studio under Ettore Sottsass. He has also worked in partnership with Giorgio Marianelli but for the past 15 years has been active independently. Barbieri is now best known for his popular product designs for Rexite.

Designed with Anna Giuffrida, his Paper Chair has a seat composed of two identical bent-plywood sections. The name was chosen because the shell is folded much like a piece of paper. The idea was inspired, says Barbieri, by "the 'Heaven and Hell' origami game I used to play

with when I was a child."

The junction feature of the two identical shell sections underwent a vast number of trials at the hands of Plank's technicians. The connecting method finally adopted is technically innovative.

When the chair was first placed on sale, the shell was mainly produced in a single color and in one material. Eventually, the various chair configurations became available in a significantly widened range.

The shell permits the attachment of various bases and, in its straight-legged version, is stackable.

Other maquettes, testing, and production follow >

1. A prototype to develop the leg configuration. This solution was eventually changed.

2. A further experiment with the leg configuration to arrive at the chair's stackability. The shell here is that of the solution finally adopted.

3. An experiment with the arms, which were later attached to the metal swivel base.

4–5. An early version featured an overlapping connection for the two-part shell—it was ultimately rejected.

6. Machinery is employed to test how much stress it will take.

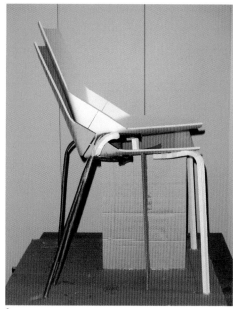

1

2

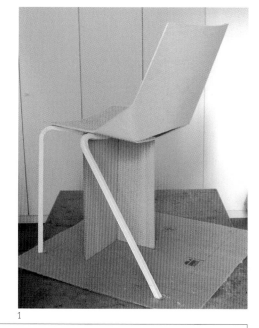

3

5

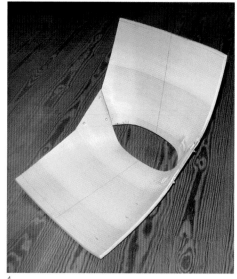

6

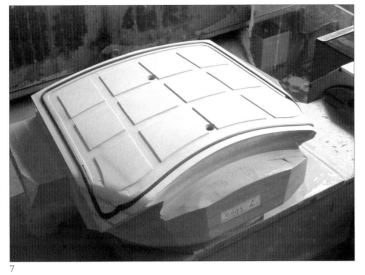

7

8

9

10

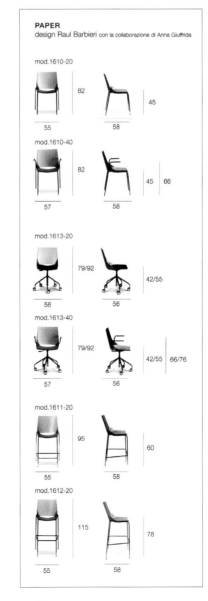

PAPER
design Raul Barbieri con la collaborazione di Anna Giuffrida

mod.1610-20

82 · 45 · 55 · 58

mod.1610-40

82 · 45 · 66 · 57 · 58

mod.1613-20

79/92 · 42/55 · 56 · 56

mod.1613-40

79/92 · 42/55 · 66/76 · 57 · 56

mod.1611-20

95 · 60 · 55 · 58

mod.1612-20

115 · 78 · 55 · 58

7. The bottom element of the die for the press-bending by heat of each of the two sections of the plywood shell. Since the two sections of the shells are the same, only one two-part die is required.

8. One of the two sections of the veneered plywood seat has been shaped.

9. A worker attaches the two-piece seat using the specially developed machinery and pins.

10. A close view of the stacking solution.

11. A catalogue presentation of the range of available configurations excludes any reference to the wide range of veneers and color combinations.

11

1. Two of the first-trial molded sections were assembled to test the shape and strength.

2. One side of the mold for the backrest and back legs.

3. The mold for the seat and front legs in its closed position.

4. A demonstration of the soft nature of the R606 polymer.

5. Though the shape might suggest otherwise, the flexing back offers ergonomic qualities.

6. Six stacked examples in six different colors.

2

1

3

4

5

6

R606 Uno Stacking Side Chair

Designers	Bartoli Design (Albertina Amadeo, b. 1932; Anna Bartoli, b. 1963; Carlo Bartoli, b. 1931; Paolo Bartoli, b. 1968; Paolo Crescenti, b. 1966; Giulio Ripamonti, b. 1952) and Fauciglietti Engineering (Renzo Fauciglietti, b. 1941; Graziella Bianchi, b. 1946)
Manufacturer	Segis S.p.A., Poggibonsi (SI), Italy
Date of design	2003
Materials	Peripheral skeletal frame: steel; covering: molded double-density R606 polymer
Size (mm/in.)	480/18⅞ wide, 790/31⅛₆ high, 450/17¾ deep, 440/17⅞₆ seat height

The Bartoli Design studio was founded in 1999. Renzo Fauciglietti and Graziella Bianchi established Fauciglietti Engineering in 1989.

The two entities have collaborated with the manufacturer Segis to create a chair that is more sophisticated technically than its simple appearance might suggest. Fauciglietti initiated the project; the Bartoli group rendered the design; both engineered it.

The technique of double injection molding a hard and a soft material has been pursued for a number of years in the production of small objects—Santoprene® for the part-

soft, part-firm handles of ski poles, for instance. However, R606 is different.

The R606 Uno Chair is the first object to test the potential of this new soft polymer. Its special characteristic is that, when molded, it forms a surface skin composed of solid, high-specific-weight cells while inside it is soft. It has not previously been available to the furniture industry, though self-skinning plastics have.

The two sections of the chair's metal frame are injection-overmolded with the R606 material, whose outer skin and inner soft support are instantly adhered or melded.

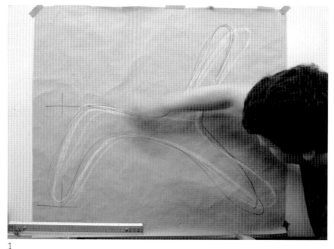

1

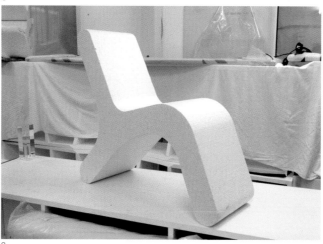

2

1. The designer develops the initial silhouette.

2. A computer rendering.

3–4. A full-size prototype in styrofoam (3) followed a miniature prototype in corrugated cardboard (4).

5. The machinery cuts and trims examples, available in an almost infinite number of color combinations. The chair can also be made in various widths.

3

4

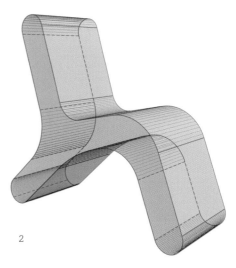

5

Foomy Chair

Designer	Markus Benesch (German, b. 1969)
Manufacturer	Moneyformilan G.b.R., Munich, Germany
Date of design	2002
Materials	Polyethylene (PE) foam and ethylene vinyl acetate (EVA) foam
Size (mm/in.)	Width varies, 670/26⅜ high, 750/29½ deep, 400/15¾ seat height

A designer with a studio in Munich serving a cadre of international clients, Benesch came upon his idea for a lightweight chair in a circuitous manner.

As he relates: "I was a bit tired of packing, unpacking, repacking heavy exhibition pieces. I wished they were made of a different material, and I could just throw them in a truck and, when I opened the trunk again, they would pop out and be ready for display.

"Looking at my sneaker sole, I had the idea of employing PE foam as the main material." He then developed the idea of creating "a chair which is easy to handle

and comfortable and also radiates an optimistic aura"
wherever it is used.

Concerning his use of foam, Benesch says: "[It]
fascinates and intrigues me tremendously at the moment.
Typically used for flip-flops [shoes] or as sneaker soles,
I am amused by the fact that I can throw these pieces
around and they won't break, even when I move my stuff
for the tenth time. It won't make any difference to them."

Benesch's foam chair—lightweight, buoyant in water,
unbreakable, available in a wide color range, and soft—
"can't hurt you—no hard edges," he asserts.

1

2

3

1–3. In May 2004, Benson constructed an example of his chair on a chromium-plated frame originally intended to hold cushions on the chair created by Le Corbusier, Jeanneret, and Perriand.

Naked Confort Club Chair

Designer	John Angelo Benson (British, b. 1971)
Manufacturer	The designer
Date of design	2004
Materials	Hay and Petit Confort Chair frame by Cassina
Size (mm/in.)	770/30⁵⁄₁₆ wide, 670/26⅜ high, 700/27⁹⁄₁₆ deep

British designer and artist Benson studied architecture under Peter Cook at the Bartlett School of Architecture, University College London, and worked in the studio of Ettore Sottsass.

For his Naked Confort chair, Benson reconnoitered the frame of a Petit Confort chair designed by Le Corbusier, Pierre Jeanneret, and Charlotte Perriand in 1928.

The resulting design is part of his Corrupted Classics Collection, which also includes his Mies Lobby Trap, based on Ludwig Mies van der Rohe's 1929 Barcelona

Chair. This features 24 sharp stainless-steel spikes protruding from its leather cushions.

The hay bales stuffed into the frame of the Naked Confort chair make it more inviting as a seat than the Mies Lobby Trap. But it is unlikely that anyone would wish actually to sit on it. The chair is more of a philosophical statement than a functional object.

Concerning the Naked Confort, Benson has written: "In a parody of the Petit Confort's exposure of its frame and as a corruption of Modernism's ideology for 'the truth to materials,' I've metaphorically revealed the interiority of the leather cushions, as leather comes from cows and they eat grass and hay!

"But more importantly today is that the notion of truth to materials has been corrupted and broken away from the modernist ideal. We now have man-made materials that look and feel like natural ones—so much so that it's virtually impossible to tell them apart. The material has become more than material! It reminds me of the film *Blade Runner* when Dr. Tyrell says to Deckard: 'More human than human is our motto at the Tyrell Corporation.'"

1–8. The designer built the wooden frame as a 1:4 scale model. Katrin Schröder, who is the head of the wicker department at the Berlin Blindenanstalt, did the weaving.

9. The first full-size prototype was in painted synthetic rattan. The designer welded the frame himself, which he then had powder-coated. The wickerwork prototype was done by specialists in Paderborn. The final version is white.

90° Straight Chair/Bench

Designer	Sven-Anwar Bibi (German, b. 1971)
Manufacturer	Blindenanstalt von Berlin, Germany
Date of design	2002
Materials	Powder-coated steel tubing, beech feet, synthetic white rattan
Size (mm/in.)	500/19¹¹⁄₁₆ wide, 1040/40⁹⁄₁₆ long

In 1998, Oliver Vogt and Hermann Weizenegger initiated the DIM (Die Imaginäre Manufaktur) concept. Under the auspices of DIM, originally directed by Peter Bergmann, a group of accomplished designers have since been commissioned to create high-design products, including furniture, that can be made by the 20 blind, low-sighted, or otherwise physically challenged artisans at the Blindenanstalt (institute for the blind) in Berlin.

"Life has infused the old rooms of the Blindenanstalt. Since DIM was established, it isn't just customers from the immediate local area who visit the Blindenanstalt shop,

Photo: Stefan Korte, Berlin

with its heavy counters and shelves dating back to the 1920s, but also new customers from around the world," Roswitha Hensel, managing director of the institute, has observed.

Bibi, a designer active in Bad Tölz, Germany, attended a workshop called Wickerworks organized by Vogt + Weizenegger to further the commendable DIM effort.

Based on a design he had previously created for a chair/bench, Bibi and the head of the institute's wicker-works department constructed a one-quarter-size model that was eventually translated into a full-size unit

made by the workers employed by the institute.

Realization of the piece followed a journey from the creation of the design in Bibi's studio with the small-scale model made in Berlin to the first-prototype steel frame welded in Düsseldorf with its wicker woven in Paderborn.

Bibi's 90° Straight Chair/Bench concept rejects traditional notions about rattan furniture, which generally features big radiuses and organic forms. By way of contrast, his chair/bench has sharp edges and angles, facilitated by the steel frame. Sitting is possible on both sides, and it is approachable from either of two directions.

1. A factory demonstration reveals the lightweight nature of the injection-molded polypropylene material—in this case, four sections or, as the designers calls them, "slices."

2. Sections are ready for low-cost shipment.

3. A seating unit composed of 12 sections.

4. A computer rendering reveals the male side (left) and the female side (right). Attachment is through force-fitting: screws or glue are therefore unnecessary. The continuous wall section is only 30 mm/1³⁄₁₆ in. thick. To build a chair, you need to connect four sections, a sofa eight, a half-round 24, and a fully enclosed circle 48.

1

2

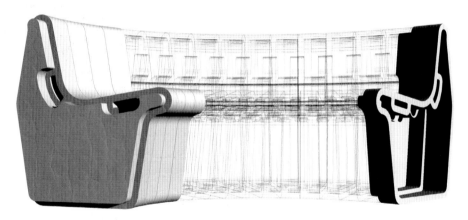

3

4

Mogu Not So Soft Seating

Designer	Stephen Burks (American, b. 1969)
Manufacturer	Ebisukasei Co., Ltd., Osaka, Japan
Date of design	2003
Materials	Injection-molded polypropylene
Size (mm/in.)	762/30 high, 659/25¹⁵⁄₁₆ deep, 465/18⁵⁄₁₆ seat height at front edge

Burks studied product design at the Institute of Design in Chicago and architecture at Columbia University, before setting up his own design/production studio, Readymade Projects, in New York in 1997.

He has worked for a number of prominent clients, such as Cappellini and Missoni. Ebisukasei itself is little known, although its Mogu pillows are famous.

The Mogu Not So Soft Seating takes its name from the Mogu collection of soft pillows that are tightly packed with polystyrene pellets. The chair is formed from injection-molded polypropylene pellets.

"The goal was to use the minimum amount of material in a single mold to yield a single part, which, used in combination with itself, could form a new chair typology," Burks acknowledges.

He developed the seating in two months—from initial sketch to the prototypes, which he showed at the 2003 Salone del Mobile (furniture fair) in Milan, Italy.

Essentially a modular seating system, each identical section includes a male connection on one side and a female on the other. The sections are pressed into each other—no screws or adhesive required.

1

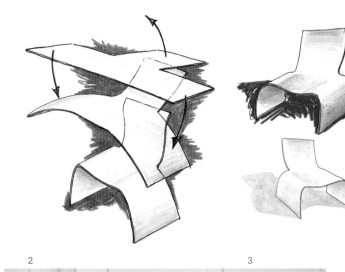

4

6

2

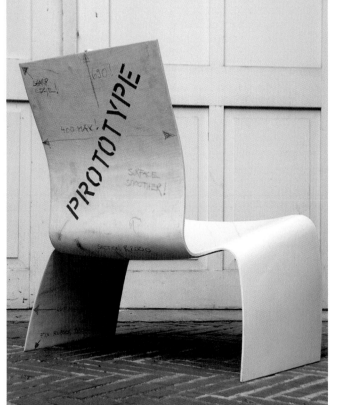

3

5

1. At the beginning of the design process, miniature cut-paper mock-ups were used to explore the possibilities of shape.

2. The simple form—a two-dimensional "T" shape—is bent into a three-dimensional chair.

3. Initial drawings of the final "T"-plan solution.

4. The designers offer this image of floating newspaper to illustrate the inspiration behind the chair.

5. A full-size prototype was built. Various notations were made on it as instructions for further refinement.

6. Made of fiberglass and with a gel-coated surface, the chair is appropriate for outdoor use. (The Lollipop Lamp of 2002 is a büro für form design produced by Vibia.)

Flight Lounge Chair

Designers	büro für form: Benjamin Hopf (German, b. 1971) and Constantin Wortmann (German, b. 1970)
Manufacturer	Habitat UK Ltd., London, UK
Date of design	2002
Materials	Hand-laminated fiberglass and epoxy resin, gel-coat finishing
Size (mm/in.)	Overall: 715.2/28³⁄₁₆ wide, 683/26⅞ high, depth varies with flex

In Germany, Benjamin Hopf worked at Siemens and Constantin Wortmann in the design studio of lighting designer/manufacturer Ingo Maurer before setting up a studio together in Munich. Their work includes furniture, lighting, and housewares.

The Flight Chair realizes their goal of creating a chair that is very light in appearance—that is, in their words, "almost flying, like a newspaper bending in the wind."

"We had to do very many paper mock-ups to find the ideal curved shape. Fiberglass is perfect for the design [because it can be made] very thin, extremely stable [with]

Photo: David Steets

smooth curves in an organic form, and waterproof for outside use."

Even though fiberglass may not be light in weight, the inexpensive Flight Chair nevertheless projects an appearance of lightness. Its actual weight suggests substance and value.

The concept well satisfies the mandate of manufacturer/retailer Habitat. The firm sells its products through more than 70 of its own stores in the UK, France, Germany, and Spain. Its young clientele has a predilection for well-designed, low-cost home furnishings.

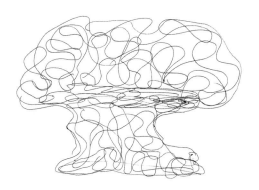

1

2

3

5

4

1. A late-1980s drawing by Humberto Campana of an idea for an iron sculpture was transformed into an armchair 13 years later. The inspiration was sea coral.

2–3. Experimentation began with bent and welded, but linear, wire elements.

4. A subsequent prototype lacks the still-to-be-determined base.

5. A denser, more free-form model, occupied by Humberto Campana, is nearer to the final version.

Corallo Armchair

Designers	Humberto Campana (Brazilian, b. 1953) and Fernando Campana (Brazilian, b. 1961)
Manufacturer	Edra S.p.A., Milan, Italy
Date of design	1989–2003
Materials	Electrostatically spray-painted steel wire, individually hand- and tool-formed and welded
Size (mm/in.)	Approx. 1000/39⅜ wide, 800/31½ high, 1200/47¼ deep (each example slightly different)

Humberto Campana studied law, and Fernando Campana architecture in their native São Paulo, Brazil. They eventually turned to design and have since become well known, their work starting to appear in European design magazines from about 1994.

The Corallo Armchair joins a range of Campana designs rooted in the interpretation of ordinary pre-existing materials. The idea for the Corallo (the Portuguese word for coral) was born in 1989 when Humberto was working on an iron sculpture as part of a plastic-arts course.

The exercise resulted in a spontaneous drawing, based

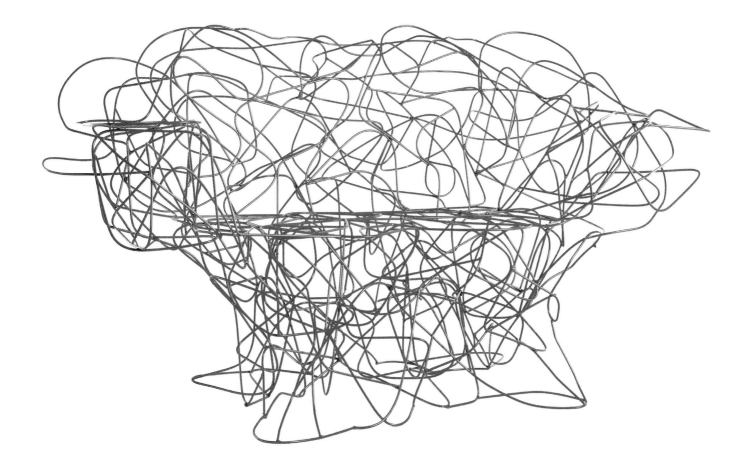

on sea coral, that dematerialized lines in space.

Massimo Morozzi, the artistic director of manufacturer Edra, had already commissioned a number of designs from the Campanas before he recognized in 2003 that the coral drawing could be developed into an armchair.

Morozzi has been instrumental, both through Edra and as a journalist, particularly for *Abitare* magazine, in bringing international attention to the brothers' work.

He encouraged the Campanas to pursue the Corallo concept. They developed a series of full-scale models, transposing a two-dimensional idea into three dimensions.

In fact, the photograph of the armchair shown above might be mistaken for a drawing. But the final armchair is rather different and more spontaneous than the prototypes realized in São Paulo.

Edra, an enlightened manufacturer known for its cutting-edge furniture, produces the Corallo Armchair more in the spirit of editions of unique models than of standardized mass production. The handmade chairs are all somewhat different from one to another, as the integrity of the original concept demands. The price of a chair is accordingly high.

1. One of the designer's charcoal sketches.

2. The mold is coated with a gel that permits easy removal of the final poly-ester resin-and-fiberglass form.

3. Over the gel, a fabricator adds a coat of polyester resin. This is highly toxic, hence the face mask.

4. After applying the polyester resin, the fabricator covers the form with fiberglass.

5. In his own workshop, Campbell laminates a dress-weight fabric using polyester resin as an adhesive.

6. After the lamination and the resin cures, the excess fabric that extends over the edges is trimmed away.

Eudora Club Chair

Designer	Critz Campbell (American, b. 1967)
Manufacturer	B9 design llc, West Point, Mississippi, US
Date of design	2002
Materials	Fiberglass, glue, printed dress-weight fabric
Size (mm/in.)	787/31 wide, 914/36 high, 787/31 deep

American designer Critz Campbell, a native of Mississippi in the southeast of the US, studied at a number of institutions—in his home state; Chicago; Lisbon, Portugal; Penland, North Carolina; and the UK—before finally settling in Chicago.

Each Eudora Club Chair is produced by professional fabricators and finished by Campbell. Its unique feature is the inner light. The designer says: "Each chair is made by hand to ensure serendipity and beauty… [and] illuminated from within to create an enticing and surreal object."

The chair, also available as a love seat (1295 mm/

51 in. wide, 914 mm/36 in. high, 787 mm/31 in. deep), has received wide exposure in the US press and on TV and was included in the 2003 "Inside Design Now" triennial at the Cooper-Hewitt National Design Museum in New York.

Being named for the Mississippi writer and photographer Eudora Welty (1909–2001) and with its traditional shape and kitsch range of patterned fabrics, the chair evokes a certain nostalgia. Other fabrics can also be specified by the customer, though one of Campbell's own selection would be more appropriate to the historically referenced concept.

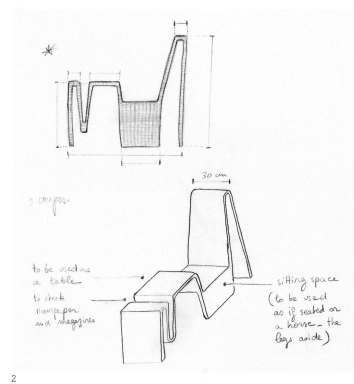

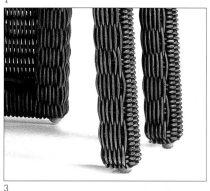

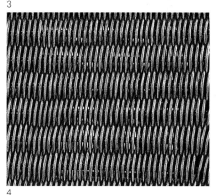

1. A wild array of rattan stalks, in their natural state before staining, is under the full control of the Javanese weavers even though it may appear otherwise. (See Mark Gutjahr's JalanJalan Stacking Chair, pp. 92–93, also woven in Indonesia by the same manufacturer.)

2. The designer's initial sketch.

3–4. Close views of the stained rattan woven over the wooden frame.

5. The seat in use. (The person in the photograph is not the designer.)

Spaces Stackable Seat

Designer	Karen Chekerdjian (Lebanese-Armenian, b. 1970)
Manufacturer	Mande, Bogor, West Java, Indonesia
Date of design	2003
Materials	Wood and rattan
Size (mm/in.)	400/15¾ wide, 960/37¹³⁄₁₆ high, 1400/55⅛ deep, 350/13¾ seat height, 500/19¹¹⁄₁₆ work-surface height, 300/11¹³⁄₁₆ width of frame

Chekerdjian was born in Beirut and studied film in Paris and design at the Domus Academy in Milan, Italy. After working in advertising, in 1993 she founded with two associates the Mind the Gap communications and graphic-design agency in Beirut. She is currently active in Amman, Jordan.

This seating unit was the first of a group of objects she calls Spaces. Chekerdjian recounts: "The lounge chair was designed during my first weeks living in Jordan. Forced to live in a hotel room for a month, I had to define a space for myself so I could feel 'at work.' With my portable

Photos: Nadim Asfâr (p. 41; p. 40, bottom row)

computer as a best friend, I experienced many different
areas in the hotel. From bedroom to lobby, I tried every
single place I could to sit in. The lounge chair was
an unconscious response to the situation. I thought of
the seat as my personal space, even if I were sitting
in public."

She explains: "You sit on it as if you are riding a
horse. You place your tray or computer on the table. And
you put your books and magazines in the slit."

This unit for eating, drinking, reading, or working on
was built by Asian artisans using indigenous materials.

1–2. The designer's playful concept sketches.

3. The seat is available in a range of transparent and solid-colored PVC materials. The two sheets of an arm are simultaneously cut and heat-fused by a machinery press that acts much like a waffle iron.

4–5. An adult and a child demonstrate its appeal to different age groups and its indoor/outdoor use.

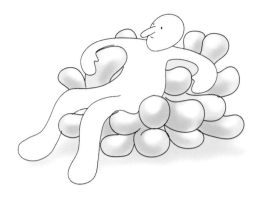

1

2

5

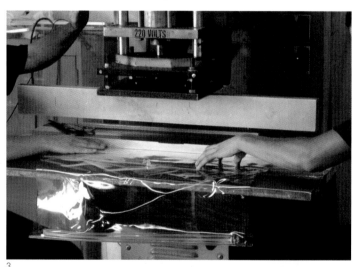

3

4

Uni Chair

Designer	Tung Chiang (Chinese, b. 1966)
Manufacturer	Bozart Toys, Inc., Philadelphia, Pennsylvania, US
Date of design	2002
Materials	15-gauge polyvinylchloride (PVC) sheeting, foot-operated floor pump
Size (mm/in.)	1220/48 dia., 431/17 each arm length radiating from a central balloon

The designer was born in Hong Kong, where he studied architecture at the Polytechnic; he became active in advertising and then went on to study furniture design at the Art Center College of Design in Los Angeles. He established a studio in California in 2002.

Inspired by inflatable and beanbag seats of the 1960s, the Uni is named for the Japanese word for sea urchin. It is produced by Bozart, a firm that specializes in products that appeal to both children and adults, such as contemporary doll's houses.

Chiang admits: "I love to do unexpected things with

food. In this vein I thought that a sea urchin might make a wonderful seat.

"Rather than having the urchin sit on top of limbs of rice like a piece of sushi, I thought maybe we could try to sit on *it* instead. This inflatable sea urchin allows you to sit on it at any angle or in any position you like. In the same way that really good chefs can surprise our eyes and tastebuds by coming up with new ways of treating food, so can a good designer too."

Three dozen arms, or legs, radiate from a central ball. It is purchased flat and inflated with a foot pump.

1–2. Studies were conducted for a solution to the metal superstructure and its attachment to the shell.

3. Molding a seat shell, here in blackwood veneer. (Moccawood is also available.)

4. The first stage of molding, before the shell periphery is cut.

5. An exotic-wood veneer (here moccawood) is applied to both front and back surfaces.

6. The tight-stacking configuration.

7. It is available in a height-adjustable caster-fitted model and as a side chair with arms (not shown) or without.

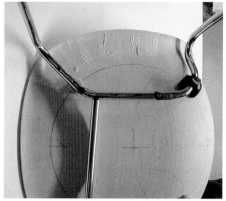
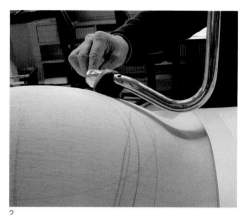

1

2

3

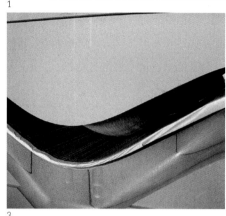

4

5

6

7

Luna Chair

Designers	Biagio Cisotti (Italian, b. 1955) and Sandra Laube (Italian, b. 1967)
Manufacturer	Plank Collezioni S.r.l., Ora (BZ), Italy
Date of design	2002
Materials	Molded plywood (blackwood or moccawood veneers) and chromium-plated or satin-finished stainless-steel superstructure
Size (mm/in.)	Standard side chair with straight legs: 580/22¹³⁄₁₆ wide, 850/33½ high, 600/23⅝ deep, 850/33½ seat height

Cisotti studied architecture in Florence and was the art director of Poltrona Frau. Since 1997, he has been the art director at Plank, the manufacturer of Barbieri's Paper Chair. Laube, who currently works with Cisotti in Florence, studied at a number of institutions in Italy and the US.

The Luna Chair is testament to the predilection of Italian manufacturers, in this case Plank, for collaborating with accomplished designers and conducting research into the development of sophisticated technological solutions for furniture production with high-design principles. (See Barbieri's Paper Chair, pp. 20–23.)

The technicians at Plank pursued the development of a new approach to plywood, initiated by Cisotti and Laube's earlier Millefoglie Chair, which has a two-part seat. The resulting material has a reduced weight of up to 60% compared to molded plastic or metal with the same strength.

Luna's striped wood pattern emphasizes its volume. The chair received the Interior Innovation Award at the 2004 Internationale Möbelmesse (furniture fair) in Cologne and the 2004 Best of Neocon® Innovation Award in Chicago.

1

2

3

4

1. The façade of the Sfera Building in Kyoto, a pre-existing structure renovated by Claesson Koivisto Rune Arkitektkontor A.B.

2. A glass-pane mock-up illustrates the light-casting nature of the leaf pattern.

3–4. Near their Stockholm architecture studio, the designers picked some cherry leaves and laid them out on a light table in a somewhat random pattern. They photographed the pattern digitally, and the image was used as the template for piercing the titanium panels of the building's façade. Eventually, the pattern was called on for the Sfera Chair.

Sfera Chair

Designers	Claesson Koivisto Rune Arkitektkontor A.B. (Mårten Claesson, b. 1970; Eero Koivisto, b. 1958; and Ola Rune, b. 1963); Swedish
Manufacturer	Ricordi & Sfera Co., Ltd., Kyoto, Japan
Date of design	2003
Materials	Seat: 1.2 mm/¹⁄₁₆ in. painted sheet steel; legs: 19 mm/¾ in. dia. stainless-steel tubing
Size (mm/in.)	660/26 wide, 740/29⅛ high, 560/22 deep

The Claesson–Koivisto–Rune architecture/design team established a studio in 1993 and achieved initial recognition with the Vila Wabi, a temporary housing project on Sergel Square in Stockholm, the city in which the group's studio practice is located. Their work has so far won 11 Excellent Swedish Design Awards.

They have designed numerous shops, showrooms, bars, restaurants, offices, and houses, both in Sweden and elsewhere. They have created furniture and furnishings for such as Offecct, Swedese, Skandiform, David Design, Cappellini, and Boffi.

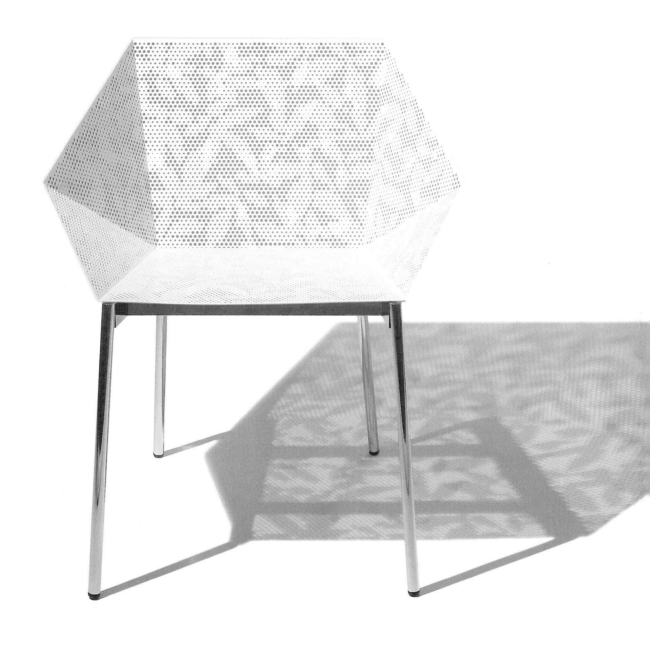

The team relates the history of the chair: "The idea... sprang from the Sfera Building, [which we renovated and that was] completed in Kyoto, Japan. The leaf-patterned façade, made by punching holes through titanium-sheet panels, filters sunlight and creates a distinct leaf-patterned shadow into the interior of the building.

"The owner, Mr. Shigeo Mashiro, wished for a chair which he could use in his outdoor café. Pleased by the effect of the façade and its shadow, we hit upon the idea of creating a chair which would also symbolize the Sfera Building by using the same idea.

"However, to achieve the punched-hole pattern, the chair's design had to begin life as a flat sheet. Inspired by origami paper-folding exercises, we developed a form which was strong, yet incredibly thin. Of only three possible companies in Japan, one company, using laser-cutting techniques, was able to manufacture the chair."

Other chairs on these pages have called on origami as a source of inspiration: examples are Agnoli's Cubica Armchair, pp. 10–11, and Barbieri and Giuffrida's Paper Stacking Chair, pp. 20–23.

Maquette and production follow >

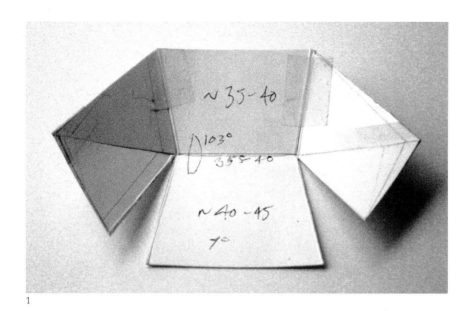

1

1. The miniature cardboard maquette is little different from the final form.

2. Sophisticated computer-numeric-controlled (CNC) machinery, operating behind protective glass, cuts out the cherry-leaf pattern.

2

3

4

3. An artisan finishes the
the surface of a flat seat
shell in sheet steel (1.2
mm/¹⁄₂₀ in. thick).

4. Two partially folded
seats await further folding
and final welding of
the arms to the seating
surface.

5. Notice that the same
workperson finishes, welds
(shown here), and
assembles the chairs.

6–7. Arc welding is also
employed for assembly of
the stainless-steel support
structure whose legs are
19 mm-/¾ in.-dia. tubing.

5

6

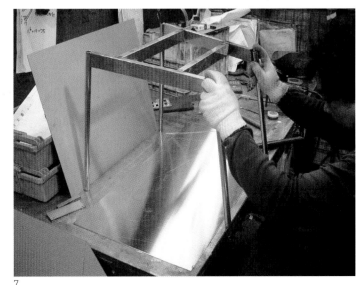

7

1

3

4

2

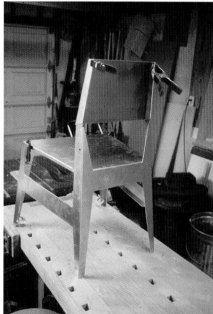

5

6

1. An exploded drawing of the four parts that are held in place with super-strength adhesive tape—no screws. The tape requires 72 hours of curing time.

2. The designer's developmental sketches.

3. Mock-ups in aluminum.

4. To arrive at the proper proportions, a corrugated-cardboard model was built.

5–6. The designer cuts out the sections with a router and templates (5) to assemble a full-size mock-up (6). Final production parts were cut with computer-directed machinery.

GC04 Side Chair

Designer	Gary Cruce (American, b. 1967)
Manufacturer	Cruce Studio, Seattle, Washington, US
Date of design	2002
Material	1.6 mm/¹⁄₁₆ in 5052 H32 aluminum-alloy sheeting and VHB™ double-coated acrylic-foam adhesive tape by 3M
Size (mm/in.)	530/28⅞ wide, 790/31⅛ high, 510/20¹⁄₁₆ deep, 430/16¹⁵⁄₁₆ seat height

Seattle-based architect/designer Cruce is known for his simple designs—for instance, a birdhouse called Nest that he originally built for his bird-watching wife and that is now in production. He has also designed chairs and stools in wood, plastic, and, as here, aluminum.

The GC04 is a mono-material chair whose strength is realized by the folds of standard-stock aluminum-alloy sheeting. The sections are cut by computer-controlled (CNC) machinery and break-press folded. The surface is polyurethane powder-coated. The parts are held in place with a special high-bonding adhesive tape.

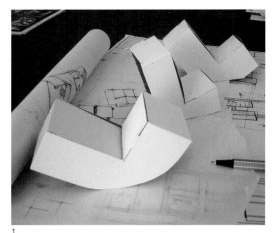

1

2

1. Initial maquettes were made, and the curve was later changed to a notch.

2. The polyurethane-foam element is cold-cured molded.

3. The foam padding and the birch plywood frame.

4. Complete and incomplete chairs. The angle where the back meets the seating surface on the wood frame, not visible on the finished chair, is the feature that offers comfort to the lower spine of the sitter.

5. Covered in a stain-resistant polyester fabric, chairs are available in red, black, blue, light gray, olive, and orange. Velcro tape attaches the upholstery.

3

4

5

Lümmel Chair

Designers	defacto.design (Nikolaus Hartl, b. 1969, and Hannes Weber, b. 1968), German
Manufacturer	Sellando GmbH, Coburg, Germany
Date of design	2002
Materials	Teflon®-coated polyester fabric, mold-cast cold-cured polyurethane foam, birch-plywood frame, Velcro fastening
Size (mm/in.)	310/12³⁄₁₆ wide, 685/27 high, 530/20⅞ deep

The diminutive, inexpensive Lümmel Chair by the defacto.design duo of Munich weighs only 7 kg/19 lbs.

The manufacturer maintains that the idea behind the chair is obvious—which it may not be—explaining that the goal was to fill the gap in the market for a comfortable and easy-to-carry seat whose "sitting area is extremely reduced so that the chair is very small and mobile… [and is usable] anywhere you want. In addition, you can build multi-colored sofas by standing Lümmels in a row. The unbelievable comfort comes from the sitting position"—which supports the lower back.

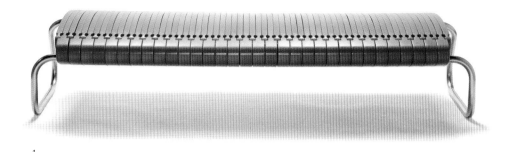

1

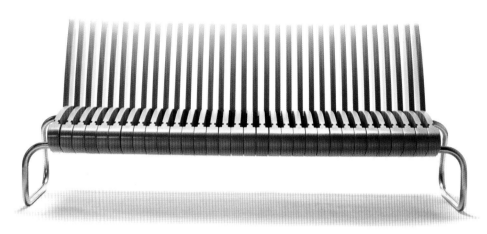

2

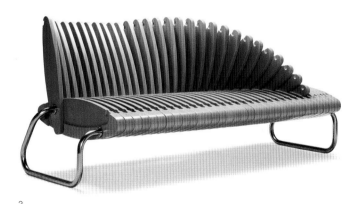

3

1. When the back lozenges are lowered into the spaces between the seat lozenges, the Double Up becomes a bench.

2. Available in three widths, the widest version is shown here. The narrowest is essentially a chair (facing page).

3. The notches at the top edge permit finger-gripping in order to lift the backrest.

Double Up Chair and Settee

Designers	The Design Laboratory (Boris Thuery and George Bigden), British
Manufacturer	Sturm und Plastic, division of La Rosa S.p.A., Palazzolo Milanese (MI), Italy
Date of design	2004
Materials	Seat: self-skinning polyurethane foam; superstructure: stainless-steel tubing
Size (mm/in.)	1250–1860/49¼–73¼ wide, 750/29⁹⁄₁₆ high, 740/29⅛ deep, 400/15¾ seat height. Each module: seat 199.16/7⅞ high, 750/29½ deep; backrest 605.75/23⅞ high, 137.63/5⁷⁄₁₆ deep

The manufacturer, which also produces furniture in metal and wood, chose to explore the structural possibilities of polyurethane foam. The result is the Double Up seating unit, composed of interlocking lozenges of the material.

In addition to serving as a tactile plaything, the unit is appropriate for sitting on, regardless of its unusual appearance. In its folded state, the seat is a bench; unfolded, it is a chair or sofa.

The designers, Boris Thuery and George Bigden, were in residency at the Sturm und Plastic factory and collaborated with the technicians on the factory floor in

order to become familiar with the production capabilities of the plant.

Two different molds cast the back and seat modules, whose dimensions are different. A locking system is molded into the bottom of the uprights so that they angle in the correct position to form the backrest. The continuous stainless-steel tubing of the superstructure is a simple, effective solution.

Bigden has recently settled in Stoke-on-Trent while Thuery, known for his unorthodox design work, is active in London. Both regularly collaborate with others.

Conceptual drawings and production follow >

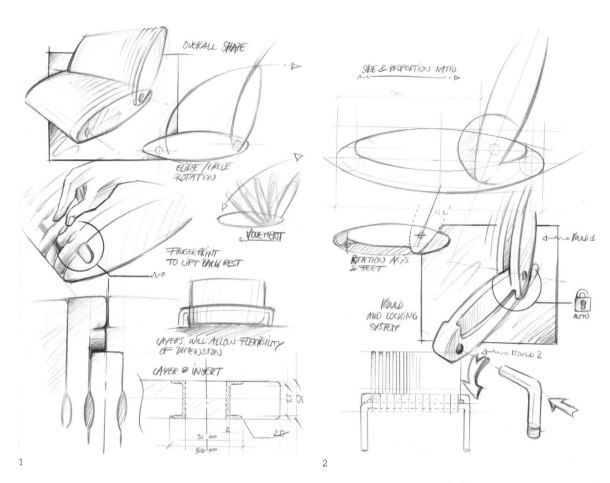

OVERALL SHAPE

ELLIPSE / CIRCLE ROTATION

MOVEMENT

FINGER PRINT TO LIFT BACK REST

LAYERS WILL ALLOW FLEXIBILITY OF DIMENSION

LAYER & INSERT

30 mm
50 mm
25
20

1

SIDE & PROPORTION RATIO

ROTATION AXIS & FEET

MOULD AND LOCKING SYSTEM

MOULD 1

MOULD 2

AUTO

2

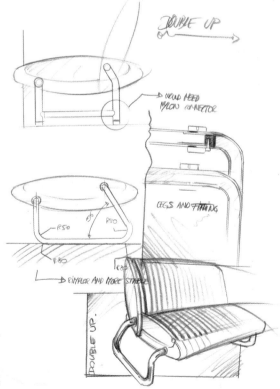

DOUBLE UP

WOULD NEED NYLON CONNECTOR

LEGS AND FITTING

R50
R50
R50
R50

SIMPLER AND MORE STABLE

DOUBLE UP

3

1–3. Sketches reveal details of the structure. Notice the "fingerprint" indentation (1) to allow the finger-lifting of the back elements and the padlock symbol (2) that points out the locking feature of the backrest lozenges.

4. The mold is sprayed so that, after being injected, the polyurethane does not stick to the surface and can be easily removed.

5. A polyurethane lozenge for the seat is removed from the mold.

6. A stock of newly formed lozenges.

7–8. Back and seat lozenges are alternately slid onto the tubular frame. White nylon rings (7) facilitate smooth rotation. Metal rings have been inserted into the holes to eliminate direct tube-to-polyurethane contact.

4

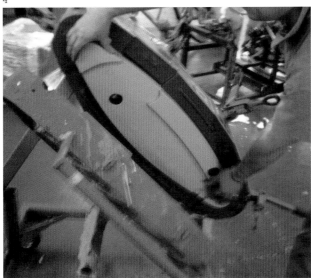

5

6

7

8

1

2

3

4

5

1. A close view of the PET copolymer, which has a glasslike appearance.

2. Within a wooden mold, an artisan winds round extruded PET rope. Gloves are necessary because the "fresh" material is hot.

3. Having formed the seat/back, an artisan completes the legs. The frosted appearance of the extrusion in the foreground changes to clear upon hardening.

4. The process was demonstrated in a street vitrine of Selfridges department store on Oxford Street in London.

5. A more ambitious sofa size is being formed using lavender-tinted plastic ropes.

Fresh Fat Easy Chair

Designer	Tom Dixon (British/French-Latvian, b. 1959)
Manufacturer	Tom Dixon (Design Research Ltd.), London, UK
Date of design	2002
Materials	Polyethylene terephtalate (PET) copolyester by Eastman Provista
Sizes (mm/in.)	560/22 wide, 700/27⁹⁄₁₆ high, 700/27⁹⁄₁₆ deep

British designer Dixon, who attended the Chelsea School of Art in London for only six months, has had a varied career, including having worked as a graphic designer, a colorist for animated films, and a performance artist. Today he is the head of his own design firm and the creative director of Habitat.

With the Fresh Fat Easy Chair, Dixon wants to challenge the commercial pattern of the production of cheap plastic objects made in very large quantities, primarily by large firms. With the Fresh Fat seat, he hopes to restore respect to the plastic object.

Each chair, formed by hand, has a different pattern. Hot, "fresh," "fat" polymer is extruded much like sausage and freely arranged over a wooden form. The robust PET ropes look more like glass than plastic.

The Fresh Fat East Chair is expensive. Dixon himself placed a prototype of a similarly formed chaise longue in the auction at Phillips, de Pury & Company in New York on June 10, 2004 for an estimated price of $14,000–$16,000.

The extruded-plastic process has been extended to other Dixon designs such as lighting and tabletop and larger seating items.

1. Shira Drach uses a drill press in her father's studio to make one of the chair miniatures for an exhibition at her school. She began with preliminary pencil drawings. In the show, the drawings were juxtaposed with the miniatures.

2. From the drawings, she and her father developed three-dimensional manifestations of her friends' preferences. The example in Ami Drach's hand expresses "Abigail likes McDonald's french fries" (also facing page, top left). And one of the chairs reveals Shira's own interests—drawing and sketching (see facing page, lower left). The project took three months to complete.

2

Drach Seats

Designers	Shira Drach (Israeli, b. 1995) and Ami Drach (Israeli, b. 1963)
Manufacturer	Unique pieces by the designers
Date of design	2003
Materials	Various
Size (mm/in.)	Approx. 70/2¾ wide, 100/3¹⁵⁄₁₆ high, 70/2¾ deep

Shira Drach is the daughter of Ami Drach, a professional Israeli designer who is the head of the industrial-design department of the Bezalel Academy in Jerusalem.

She was a fourth-grader in the Balfour Elementary School in Tel Aviv when she and her father built entries for the exhibition "A Chair for Each Child," which was part of a special parent-child art project.

Shira interviewed friends at the school to discover what they liked most. Inspired by the small maquettes she had seen in her father's studio and to illustrate her friends' preferences, she and he built miniature chairs.

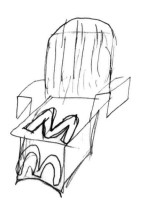

Abigail likes McDonald's french fries.

Daniel likes to paint.

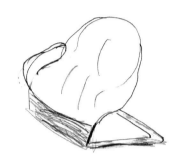

Hagar likes hearts.

Itamar likes boxing.

Maayan likes to eat.

Neal likes computer games.

Shira likes to draw and sketch.

Tomer likes karate.

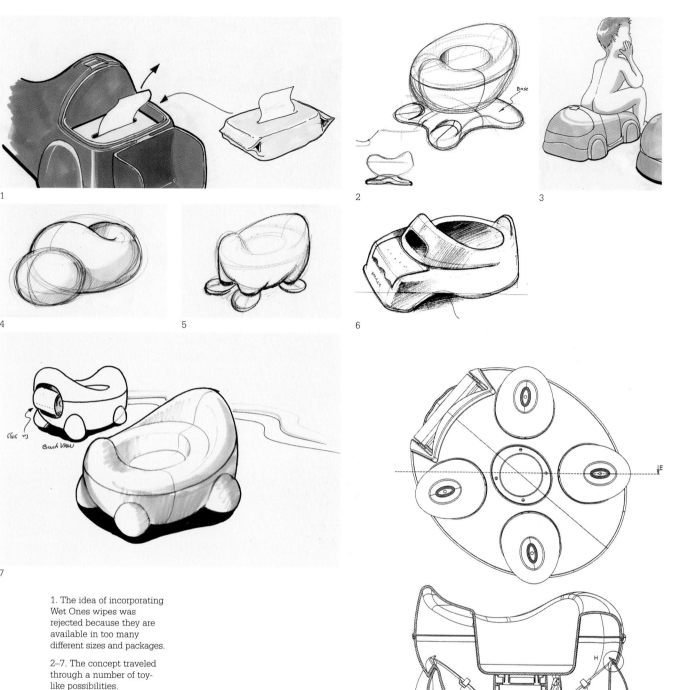

1. The idea of incorporating Wet Ones wipes was rejected because they are available in too many different sizes and packages.

2–7. The concept traveled through a number of toy-like possibilities.

8. A technical drawing of the ultimate solution—a two-part chassis and four feet in molded polypropylene.

Baby-Bug Potty Chair

Designers	Boaz Drori (Israeli, b. 1968), Paul Pressman (Israeli, b. 1964), and Raanan Volk (Israeli, b. 1963) (Aran Research and Development)
Manufacturer	Odem Plast, Marigny-St.-Marcel (Haute-Savoie), France, for Kids Kit Ltd., North Golan Heights, Israel
Date of design	2002
Materials	Polypropylene
Size (mm/in.)	260/10¼ wide, 240/9⁷⁄₁₆ high, 310/12³⁄₁₆ deep

The designers collaborated with Yohanan Mageni in their studio and with engineers at the Quntz Design Studio to develop the potty chair—a toilet for children.

When they first received the commission, the designers asked themselves: "What is the most missing feature of potties today? What is the thing that could really improve the life of parents and children? Our conclusion was to make it easier for parents by combining Wet Ones wipes with the potty so that parents would not have to run to where the child was ready to use a potty.

"However, after our research, we realized that it would

be completely impossible to incorporate Wet Ones due to the variety of sizes and formats they come in. And it would end up totally unused.

"Then the idea of a toilet-paper roll came to mind, still improving mommy's/daddy's lives, and, besides, the toilet-paper roll is a standard around the world."

Almost all of today's plastic potties call on monoblock technology and, as a result, look similar. The designers took an alternative approach by creating a more charming, toylike, and comfortable form.

One day over coffee, two of the designers, Drori and Pressman, realized that the shape of the classic Lily Cup reminded them of potties of the days of their childhoods when they were still essentially metal pails.

They then began sketching ideas on a paper napkin. And, from that point, they added four legs and a saddletop to look like a plaything you ride, a form to appeal to toddlers. However, the idea of sitting on a "bug" might not be embraced by all children.

Though commissioned by Kids Kit, the potties are produced by a firm in France, where toy production is popular in the Haute-Savoie department.

1. Several layers of wooden sheets are used to create plywood over a curvaceous mold.

2. A shell is formed on a single-side mold.

3. Zbryk welds the five-piece stainless-steel base, clamped firmly on a wooden jig.

4. Connectors to hold the base to the shell are screwed in place. The dotted blue line is the nylon cord that is threaded in and out of the shell. Articulated glides are fitted into the tubular legs.

5. The nylon cord is available in a range of colors.

6. A banquette is formed when chairs are placed in tandem.

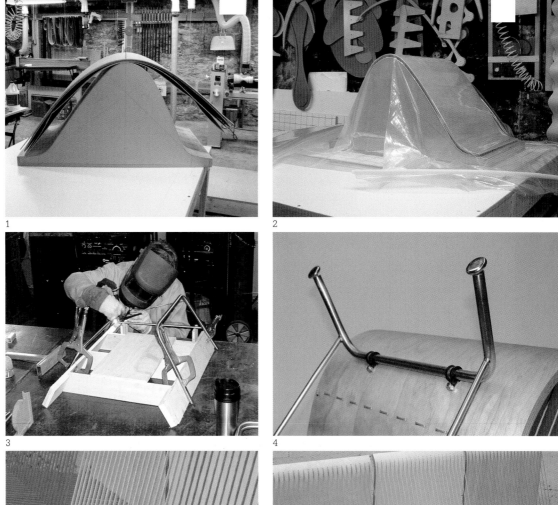

1

2

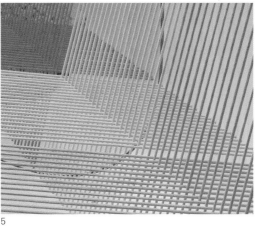

3

4

5

6

String Chair

Designers	Rie Egawa (Japanese, b. 1960) and Burgess Zbryk (American, b. 1964)
Manufacturer	Egawa + Zbryk, Kansas City, Missouri, US
Date of design	2002 prototypes, 2003 final production
Materials	Clear-lacquer-finished birch and hoop-pine veneer on plywood, welded stainless-steel tubing, nylon cord
Size (mm/in.)	560/22¹⁄₁₆ wide, 880/35⅝ high, 640/118½ deep

The work of the husband-and-wife team, active in mid-America, has been published in periodicals in the US, the UK, France, Italy, and Japan. For their work, Egawa and Zbryk have received a variety of citations, including awards at the 2001 Tokyo Designers Block, the 2001 Design Distinction Award from *I.D.* magazine, and the 2004 Charlotte Street Foundation Award.

They admit to being more interested in aesthetics than in function. In addition to plastics, metal, and paper, their work frequently exploits the potentialities of plywood—such as in the String Chair, shown here, and Puzzle Screen.

The String seat, explain the designers, "was born out of our desire to create a comfortable, lightweight chair made from a minimal amount of material.

"Devoid of any unnecessary design elements, each material [cord, wood, and metal] has a specific function," they continue.

"The nylon cord comfortably supports the sitter above the frame. And the molded plywood frame is supported by a stainless-steel base."

By placing them side by side, it is possible to produce an infinitely long banquette.

1. As the designer's sketch shows, the vacuum holders are available with double or triple cups (top left).

2. A hand vacuum cup is the standard tool of professionals who transport large and heavy panes of glass. This example by Anver, a US manufacturer (not the one used in the Wantuz chair but similar), features a lever that, when pressed down, removes air and strongly adheres to the Plexiglas.

3. The Plexiglas top of the designer's Wantuz Table (1040 mm/50 in. wide, 600 mm/24⅝ in. high, 600 mm/24⅝ in. deep) is also held by vacuum cups on each end. The Plexiglas top is heat-bent at the folds. The Plexiglas of the chair and table is 15 mm/⅝ in. thick and the steel tubing is 20 mm/¾ in. in diameter.

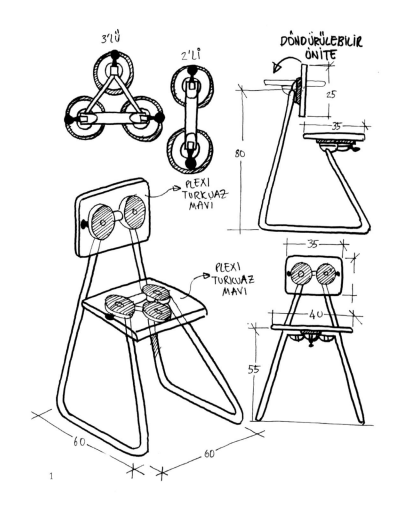

1

2

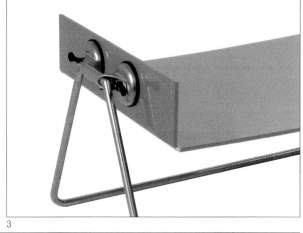

3

Wantuz Side Chair

Designer	Reha Erdoğan (Turkish, b. 1965)
Manufacturer	The designer
Date of design	2004
Materials	Hand vacuum cups, Plexiglas, tubular metal
Size (mm/in.)	600/23⅝ wide, 900/35⁷⁄₁₆ high, 600/23⅝ deep

Erdoğan has received degrees in graphic design from the İstanbul Devlet Güzel Sanatlar Akademisi (fine-arts academy) and in fine art from Mimar Sinan Üniversitesi. He began his career working at *Nokta* magazine and became a partner of Salih Memecan, a design company in Mart Ajans. Currently, he is art director of *Hürriyet*, an Istanbul daily newspaper.

He has also become adept at product design, and the "cm. Light" table lamp that incorporates a folding ruler (thus, "cm." for "centimeters") has been widely published.

Of the Wantuz Side Chair, Erdoğan says that its

"inspiration came alive when I was visiting Bauhaus, a store in Istanbul. I came to realize how functional and very practical glass-holding vacuums are and that they can hold considerable weight.

"Using colorful Plexiglas pieces, I designed a chair and a coffee table without any screws, using only plate-glass-holding vacuums. These devices give you the freedom to change the colors in seconds whenever you get bored…. With conventional furniture, we do not have the luxury to make such quick and practical changes."

The vacuum cups are used by professional glaziers.

1

2

3

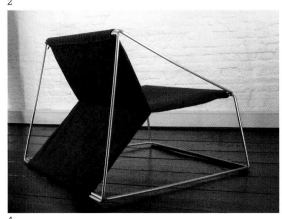

4

The chair was designed in two basic models: one with four rectangular tubular elements and another with three rectangular elements.

1–3. The tripartite reinforced fabric is zipper-fitted onto the frame. A fabric with a stretch fiber is not necessary.

4. Back view of the splayed upholstery.

There are two sizes: the lounge chair (right) and the armchair (facing page).

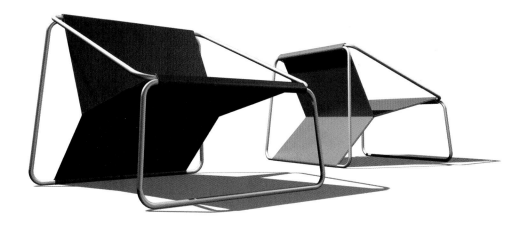

SP (Stretched Planes) Armchair and Lounge Chair

Designer	Khodi Feiz (Iranian, b. 1963)
Manufacturer	Khodi Feiz Studio, Amsterdam, Netherlands
Date of design	2002
Materials	Zippered and reinforced nonstretch fabric, stainless-steel tubing
Size (mm./in.)	Version 1 (red): 520/20½ wide, 660/26 high, 550/21⅝ deep; version 2 (gray or green): 700/27⁹⁄₁₆ wide, 620/24⁷⁄₁₆ high, 700/27⁹⁄₁₆ deep

Feiz, who was born in Teheran, studied industrial design in the US at Syracuse University subsequent to working at the Texas Instruments Design Center. After Syracuse, he emigrated to the Netherlands, where he became the manager and senior designer in Philips's Advanced Design Group. Today he works with his wife, Anneko Feiz-van Dorsen, in their studio in Amsterdam.

Feiz's roster of primarily European clients has included Offecct, Decathlon, Loewe, Bang & Olufsen, and Alessi. His work is so simple—as seen in the PO/01 Lamp by Cappellini—that an object's function may not be obvious.

The SP (Stretch Planes) Armchair, whose function *is* clear, is likewise very simple: three or four bent tubular elements for legs and arms, and an ordinary fabric.

The sophisticated engineering holds the zippered upholstery taut. The designer says: "Using the analogy of clothing on the body, the SP chair can be easily clothed to your personal taste and easily changed to suit your ever-changing moods."

Feiz has also configured the chair in a rocking version, not shown here, in which a rectangle of tubular steel curves downward between the bottom ends of the legs.

1. The clay mold is being covered with fiberglass, up to about 6 mm/¼ in. thick, the same as in the final plastic version. The high toxicity of the materials requires a protective face mask to be worn.

2. On each side of this 6 mm/¼ in. thick copy made in the clay mold, the fiberglass parts are formed and then sand-wich-pressed under high heat (see 4, 5, and 6).

3. The inner fiberglass part is cast.

4. Having just been removed from an oven, the acrylic sheet at 160°C/ 320°F is placed inside the outer fiberglass form.

5. In the next step, the inner plastic form is slid into place.

6. The designer comments: "As you can see, it took great effort for me [in red] and three classmates to assemble the whole thing! We also used clamps [not shown] to form the acrylic. And an acrylic sheet is very difficult to form, either in a vacuum or, in this case, by sandwich-pressing."

7. The shimmering, liquidlike surface on a completed seat.

1

2

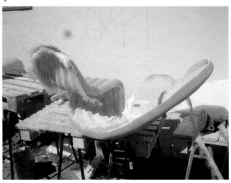

3

4

5

6

7

LapTop2 Chair

Designer	Christian Flindt (Danish, b. 1972)
Manufacturer	Production assistance from Silkeborg Plast, A.p.S., Silkeborg; Glasfibertekrik A.p.S., Copenhagen; DKI Form A.S., Spentrup; all Danish
Date of design	2002
Materials	Fiberglass version: white gel coating
Size (mm/in.)	800/31½ wide, 940/37 high, 1370/53¹⁵⁄₁₆ deep

The LapTop2 Chair is one of three seats that Flindt developed for the design colloquium "Leg Chair: Chair for the Exhibitionist" in the Department of Furniture and Design of the Arkitektskolen in Århus, Denmark.

The designer, who is interested in "form as communication," feels that furniture design is a cultural statement rather than a plastic form akin to architecture. And he thinks of it as an extension of the body in space, where the body and furniture become one.

His school project addressed the growing intrusion of sex into culture and how young people relate to their

Photo: Magnus Klitten; 3D rendering: Bo Drenov

bodies and their sexuality.

Flindt was fortunate to have three patient suppliers to assist in the project. And he turned to basic and advanced production methods and materials as well as three-dimensional-modeling computer software and lifesize photorealistic renderings.

LapTop2, in Flindt's words, "is a chair of the social arena, in which the body and the interior melt together to form one another. The chair catches and discusses social interaction in a bar [where people drink and socialize]. Traditional seating positions are mixed with playful

gestures…. To me, the potential of a new design often lies in a variation of the existing. It is the real world which makes wonderland interesting. It is classicism which made Mannerism twist out of its own ideal picture. In the same way, it is the body's knowledge of a normal chair in a bar that creates tension between the chair in the Slaughterbar." (Flindt's word "Slaughterbar" indicates a place where meat is exhibited: a bar offers a place where the voyeur and the exhibitionist come together.)

More pragmatically, the production of LapTop2 required a knowledge of the materials and technology.

1

2

1–2. The sophisticated connector is refined.

3. The male-to-female or female-to-male connectors permit infinite lengths, using two chairs and as many ottomans as desired.

4–6. Male and/or female connectors are inserted into and adhered to the foam structure of the bodies. The foam varies in thickness. The removable upholstery is available in one of three fabrics in a large range of colors.

3

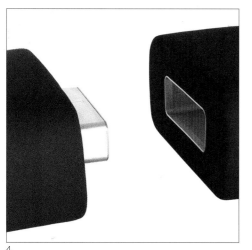

4

5

6

Sex-Fiction Lounge Chair Units

Designers	Diego Fortunato (Argentine) and Gabriel Fontanilo (Spanish, b. 1968)
Manufacturer	Ycami S.p.A., Novedrate (CO), Italy
Date of design	2004
Materials	Polyester foam and aluminum
Size (mm/in.)	Seating unit: 900/35⁷⁄₁₆ wide, 800/31½ high, 1100/43⁵⁄₁₆ deep, 380/15 seat height; ottoman unit: 900/35⁷⁄₁₆ wide, 380/15 high, 500/19¹¹⁄₁₆ deep

The designers, active in separate Barcelona studios, claim: "Sex-Fiction is based on a utopia…. Sex-Fiction Utopia is a utopian space whose inhabitants transgress all known borders between the subject and the object. Objects are freed from their passivity and reproduce themselves through sexual intercourse, thus acquiring humanoid behavior, while human beings become free of the tyranny imposed by designers and their patrons.

"The Sex-Fiction pieces of furniture fornicate just for pleasure, rather than reproduction, and, in doing so, they provide us with new uses."

The removable/interchangeable upholstery and the multiple-arrangement or "new-use" feature express a trend today that attempts to provide variety or, as some designers say, to satisfy customers' changing moods.

Fortunato, originally a sculptor, frequently focuses on designs that offer this interchangeability and use inventive methods for connecting the elements of a system. Examples, by Nani Marquina's Barcelona firm, are his Cojines! Cojines! cushions, which attach by magnetic buttons, and his Crema-Yeras rug concept, whose felt squares zipper together to create varying color patterns and sizes.

1

1. The idea for a chair leaning forward to avoid the collection of rain or snow on the seat stemmed from iconic American outdoor furniture, shown here in the designer's own backyard.

2. The unique feature of the suite is the angle interpretation of the chair's foot. The angle is the same as that of the table-leg foot.

2

Watershed Outdoor Furniture Set

Designer	Paul Galli (American, b. 1971)
Manufacturer	54Dean LLC, Brooklyn, New York, US
Date of design	2003
Materials	Mahogany (shown), white oak, or teak/stainless-steel sets, screws, waterproof polyurethane glue, wood plugs, wood biscuits, mortise/tenon construction
Sizes (mm/in.)	Chair: 406/16 wide, 813/32 high, 520/20½ deep; table: 990/39 wide, 336/15¼ high, 1524/60 deep

American designer Paul Galli has created an outdoor chairs-and-table set that invokes traditional values.

His idea is based on ubiquitous traditional outdoor wooden furniture: a slatted tabletop and a set of chairs that, when not in use, are tilted against the table to prevent rain collection. Galli's tabletop extends to protect the seats of the chairs in their leaning position.

Galli has said: "While studying photos of furniture in my backyard left in their 'natural state,' it struck me that the common act of tilting a chair against a table to shield it from the elements was actually quite charming

and beautiful. The Watershed Outdoor Furniture Set celebrates this simple, elegant solution."

With regard to the non-traditional angled foreleg, the designer acknowledges its ironical quality: "What intrigues me about this solution is that it is both whimsical and completely functional."

The angle of the chair's front leg reflects the angle of the table legs (see p. 76).

The four table legs—bolted onto the central structure of the table—are identical and removable, which negates the need to label them individually.

The table's central structure is screwed to the underside of the top.

The pieces that comprise the table top are fused with glue and biscuits. The sets in either mahogany or teak are finished with tung oil. The ensemble in the white-oak version is finished with an oil-varnish mixture.

Galli's outdoor-furniture suite makes an odd bed-fellow with the other products available in today's design world, which more often than not is interested in exploiting new materials and advanced technology.

Maquettes, drawings and production follow >

1

2

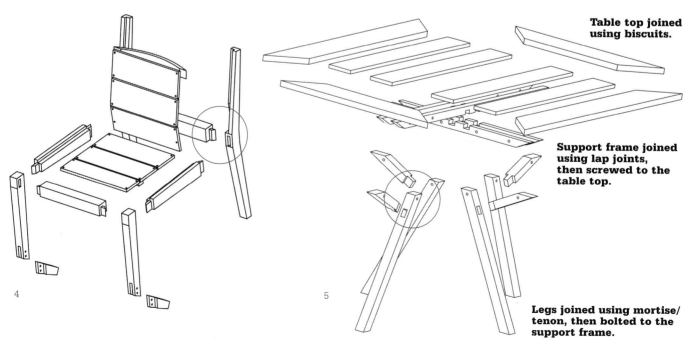

3

1–2. Small-scale models were loosely made. Styrofoam (1) and cardboard (2) were used for the tabletops.

3. A full-size mock-up followed small-scale versions.

4–5. Exploded drawings of all the parts and pieces of the chair and table. Notice the mortise-and-tenon construction (in the red circles)—male members are fitted and glued into female slots.

4

5

Table top joined using biscuits.

Support frame joined using lap joints, then screwed to the table top.

Legs joined using mortise/tenon, then bolted to the support frame.

6

7

8

6. Paper drawings are adhered for precise cutting. Leg/back pieces are shown.

7. A collection of front legs in the foreground.

8. Clamps and a jig hold the backrest in place for glue curing.

9. Traditional woodworking methods and materials, such as wood biscuits and glue, are employed. Shown here are pegs and glue.

9

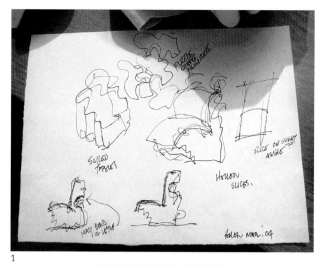

1

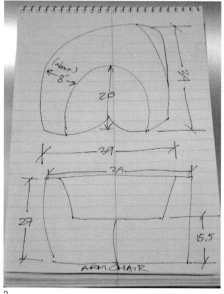

3

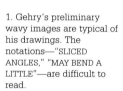

2

4

5

1. Gehry's preliminary wavy images are typical of his drawings. The notations—"SLICED ANGLES," "MAY BEND A LITTLE"—are difficult to read.

2. These drawings, even though they appear casual, provide instructions for the exact dimensions of the final sizes, here in inches.

3–5. Small solid-wood models were carved by Jeffrey Casper in Gehry's Los Angeles office. They were then digitized, increased to full size, and used to make the molds. Each item is produced by roto-molding, which permits the use of a one-side mold and objects as one piece.

Gehry Easy Chair

Designer	Frank O. Gehry (Canadian, b. 1930)
Manufacturer	Heller Incorporated, New York, New York, US
Date of design	2004
Materials	Roto-molded polymer as one piece
Size (mm/in.)	990/39 wide, 685/27 high, 860/33⅞ deep, 390/15⅜ seat height

Alan Heller, a pioneer of inexpensive high-design products in the US, commissioned the renowned architect to design the Frank Gehry Furniture Collection.

Gehry and Heller see it "as a collaboration of designing beyond what is expected and as the beginning of an exploration in new technologies."

Heller adds: "We have always striven to bring great design by great designers to a broader market with our more accessible furniture."

The Easy Chair and others pieces in the collection continue Gehry's pursuit of Deconstructivism.

1. The left-arm lever adjusts the overall height.

2. The right-arm lever adjusts the reclining angle of the backrest to occupy one of five positions.

3. The height of the arms is adjustable.

4. To reduce elbow strain, arm-pad angles can be determined within 30°–20° in and 10° out.

5. The lever beneath the seat adjusts the seat back and forth.

6. To accommodate different body shapes and seating preferences, the dial beneath the seat determines the rocking firmness.

7. Various sections are adjustable to suit individual users—ranges of 100 mm/3¹⁵⁄₁₆ in. arm height, 15 mm/⅝ in. front-to-back positions of the arm, 75 mm/2¹⁵⁄₁₆ in. for the headrest, 60 mm/2⅜ in. for the backrest, 50 mm/2 in. front-to-back position of the seat, and 120 mm/4¾ in. of the overall height.

8. A prototype includes a hard-edge back structure, an insectlike base, and an arm attached at the front end.

9. The standard model (without the headrest) is shown here and on the facing page: 95% of the materials are recyclable.

10. The mesh is available in a choice of ten mix-and-match colors.

1

2

3

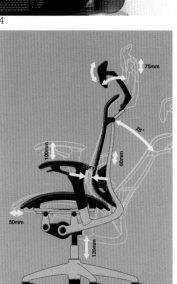
4

5

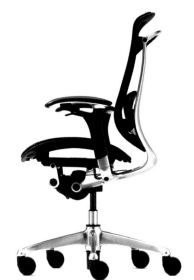
6

7

8

9

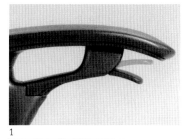
10

Contessa Office Armchair

Designer	Giugiaro Design (Italian)
Manufacturer	Okamura Corporation, Tokyo, Japan
Date of design	2002
Size (mm/in.)	Standard model: 630–730/24¹³⁄₁₆–28¾ wide, 970–1090/38³⁄₁₆–42¹⁵⁄₁₆ high, 565–615/22¼–24³⁄₁₆ deep; headrest model: 1160–1280/45¹¹⁄₁₆–50⅜ high, 565–615/22¼–24³⁄₁₆ deep; 420–560/16⁹⁄₁₆–22¹⁄₁₆ seat heights

Giorgetto Giugiaro (Italian, b. 1938) began working at age 17 with Dante Giacosa at the Fiat automobile-styling center in Turin. This was followed by work at the Bertone car bodyworks. In 1968, he established ItalDesign and, in 1981, Giugiaro Design. While best known for his car-body designs, he and others of his studio have realized numerous industrial-design commissions.

The main features of the Contessa Office Armchair are the sophisticated engineering and the transparent mesh for the back and seat.

The ergonomic features include mechanisms that

allow the user to adjust elements while seated. The
design also purports to provide comfort for office workers
who remain in the same position for long hours.

   The manufacturer conducted studies to determine the
most suitable angle, finding it to be 26°. Performance
studies were also conducted by the Giugiaro Design
group. It has been suggested that, owing to Giugiaro's
background, some of the prototypes reveal the styling of
automobiles such as the Aston Martin Twenty-Twenty
(designed by Giugiaro and his son Fabrizio) and the
ItalDesign Structura concept car.

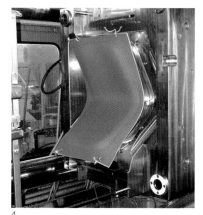

1. Exploded view of the two-part shell and the aluminum structure. The the front shell snaps into the back shell. The red dot is the handle which is covered with matching fabric.

2. Front of the mold, without the fabric.

3. The Teflon®- or polyurethane-coated fabric, with resin on the underside to prevent water absorption, awaits the closing of the mold.

4. A front shell after being pressed into shape under high heat.

5. A stack of back shells with the handles in place.

6. The two layers are force-fitted together with the aluminum frame between and held with a screw under the seat.

Only the straight-leg model, which can be stacked ten high, is shown here. Other versions have arms, caster-fitted bases, and, as a chair or a stool, a pedestal base.

Boum Chair

Designers	Monica Graffeo (Italian, b. 1973) and Ruggero Magrini (Italian, b. 1962)
Manufacturer	Kristalia S.r.l., Brugnera (PN), Italy
Date of design	2002
Materials	Back shell: injection-molded polypropylene; front element: co-injected sandwich of stain-resistant Teflon® or polyurethane-coated fabric, poly-urethane foam, and polyester interlock; frame/leg structure: aluminum or chromium-plated steel
Size (mm/in.)	Four-leg model: 610/24 wide, 790/31⅛ high, 560/22 deep, 460/18⅛ seat height at front edge

The Boum Chair was developed according to principles employed in the automobile industry for the inside of car doors, including snap-in fitting. A fabric is applied to the front shell of the chair during the molding process. The advantages are that no blisters are formed under the upholstery and no adhesive is necessary.

The fabric comes from the sports sector (in fact, for motorcyclists' jackets) and has passed high-abrasion, ripping, and pilling tests. The material, coated with either Teflon® or polyurethane, is resistant to water, abrasion, and ultraviolet rays.

About ecological concerns, the manufacturer proposes: "When you have finished using the chair, it can be dismantled by loosening the screws below the seat and the handle. In this way, it is possible to recycle the frame by taking it to the local scrap-metal recycling center. After removing the fabric cover, you will find that the lower structure and the handle are in plastic throughout and can be recycled in the polypropylene bins that are the same as those used to recycle household plastic bottles. The fabric on the handles and on the upper structure can be discarded with normal household garbage."

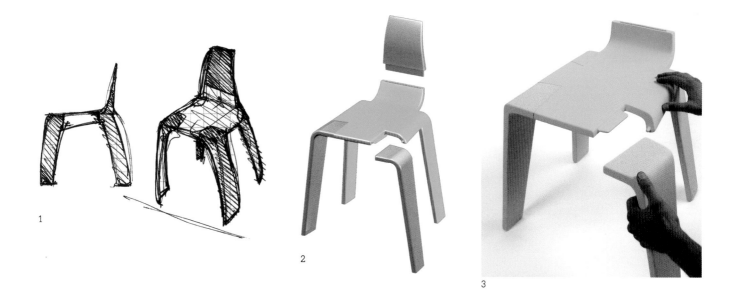

1. The designer's initial conception.

2. The six elements of the chair—the back, seat, and four legs—are snapped together.

3. A closer view reveals the attachment-joint feature.

4. The kit is purchased as two frames. The back and front legs are to be popped out of one frame and the back legs and seat from the other. The two available colors make four different combinations possible. The initial color combination can be altered at a later time to suit changing owner preferences.

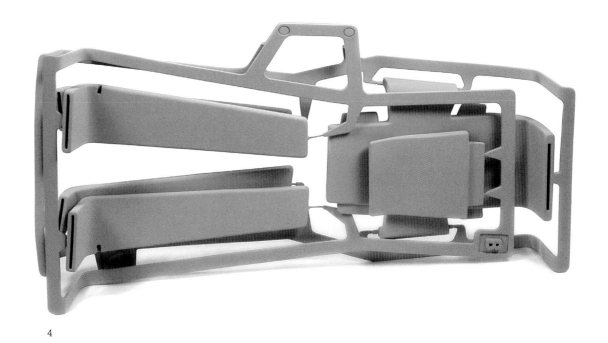

Kit Chair

Designer	Arik Grinberg (Israeli, b. 1973)
Manufacturer	The designer
Date of design	2002
Material	Polyvinylchloride
Size (mm/in.)	520/20½ wide, 700/27⁹⁄₁₆ high, 520/20½ deep

Any child who has worked with self-built plastic model kits such as those for constructing airplanes or cars will recognize the approach taken by Israeli designer Arik Grinberg for his aptly titled Kit Chair.

The elements of the chair are molded in two separate frames—the front legs and the backrest in one, the back legs and the seat in the other. The elements are popped out of the frames, the frames are discarded, and the end user snaps the elements together.

Guided by the simple, non-verbal instructions, which visually illustrate the five connection points, the user

should have no problem with the assembly process.

The plastics technology common in industrial manufacture has been applied here to furniture production. Grinberg conducted extensive experiments toward, among other solutions, the elimination of breaking or splitting at stress points.

A further aspect of the concept is its preassembled flat-stacking feature. The thin profile of the two-unit nest permits inexpensive transportation (even placement in the trunk, or boot, of an automobile) and space-saving storage (in a warehouse or the user's domicile).

The designer gave considerable thought to the color range. A user can choose from one of two colors and, if two chairs are purchased, configure—and later reconfigure —them into other combinations.

"Another element that I decided was important, one that has a value of its own, is the playful appearance of the product," the designer reveals. "Also, I think that in our era, when products are very much alike and often discarded after a short period of use, products that can be modified by users offer the opportunity for them to be active in the styling of products and give them longer lives."

1. Drinking straws are purchased in large quantities. About 15,000 are used in a single chair.

2. The designer gathers the straws for placement in the wood form.

3. From the front, a chair appears to be in one color only. The apparently random but actually rather studied placement of the second-color straws presents a side-view pattern. No two chairs feature the same side pattern.

4. When the placement of straws has been completed to the designer's satisfaction, he tightens them within the frame. He does this with an electric drill to screw together the sixth corner of the frame.

5. A heated panel is applied to the side of a chair, or the ends of the straws, melting them rigidly in place.

6. A completed chair.

1

4

2

5

3

6

Sturdy Straws Chair

Designer	Tal Gur (Israeli, b. 1962)
Manufacturer	The designer
Date of design	2002
Materials	Standard plastic drinking straws
Size (mm/in.)	Version in translucent white and orange: 330/13 wide, 710/28 high, 720/28⅜ deep

Gur, who studied industrial design at the Bezalel Academy in Jerusalem and traditional papermaking and ceramics in Japan, has explored possibilities of rotational molding not investigated by others, as well as the use of ordinary readymade materials. His Sturdy Straws Chair, simple but imaginative, is exemplary of the latter.

He considers this drinking-straw project whimsical and discloses: "The inspiration… sprouted from the local [Arab] tradition of broom-making from natural straw fiber. The fact that there are about 15,000 drinking straws combined into one chair allows for the integration of an

intricate design and color configurations. The transformation also allows for a shift from fragile, disposable drinking straws into a solid, sturdy, cheerful chair."

Even though Gur has worked with plastics manufacturers to develop new methods for the molding of plastics,
the Sturdy Straws Chair is rather low-tech.

The improvised, inexpensive make-do wood frame,
within which the straws are formed into a hexagon,
permits chairs in different sizes to be shaped with little
extra effort. The variations of the color placement make
for infinite side patterns.

1–2. Fiberglass is coated
with a bonding agent on
various individual forms
that compose the whole.

3–5. The sectional molds
are bolted together. The
seams of the fiberglass
sections are fused. The
final shape is lacquered
to produce a shiny surface
and connected to a
chromium-plated steel base.

The lamp/seat is available
in white, black, red, and
orange.

Asana Lamp/Chair

Designer	Giorgio Gurioli (Italian, b. 1957)
Manufacturer	Kundalini S.r.l., Milan, Italy
Date of design	2004
Materials	Chair column: lacquered fiberglass, chromium-plated steel; lamp diffuser: mouth-blown triple-layered Murano glass; bulb: E27 250-watt-maximum halogen bulb
Size (mm/in.)	2000/78¾ high, 600/23⅝ dia.

Gurioli is an award-winning designer who began his
career working as a planner and designer of high-tech
instruments for firms such as Digital, Motorola, Rockwell,
and Teko. Thereafter, he established his own studios:
Syn with Francesco Scansetti in 1991 and Mix Experience
in 1995.

Kundalini was founded 12 years ago by artist Gregori
Spini to produce "objects of inner illumination." The
implication is that its lamps and the light they emit
transcend the function of mere illumination and alter "our
inner selves." To express this goal, the name Kundalini, a

Sanskrit word, was chosen as the firm's name. According to yogic theory, kundalini is the life force coiled at the base of a person's spine. When aroused, it travels to the head and thence triggers enlightenment.

Asana, Sanskrit for "a steady position of the body," is the name for the system collectively known as Hatha Yoga. It is claimed that the asana posture enhances mental balance, physical strength, and flexibility.

The Kundalini firm has produced a number of lamps and pieces of furniture as separate items. The Asana represents the fusion of both.

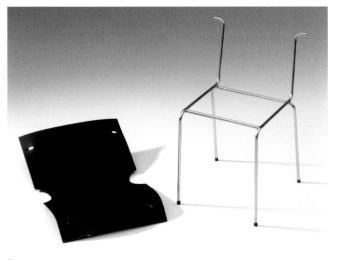

1

2

3

1. One of the two elements of the chair is the welded metal frame, which is either chromium- or electro-plated. The other is the seating surface—a one-piece plastic sheet with four holes to facilitate its being slipped over the front legs and the top hooks of the backrest.

2. A choice of two types of plastic sheeting: one is white or black PET, the other clear polycarbonate.

3. Stacked, three or more clear polycarbonate chairs would be most visually dramatic.

Flex Stacking Side Chair

Designer	Sigurdur Gustafsson (Icelandic, b. 1962)
Manufacturer	Källemo A.B., Värnamo, Sweden
Date of design	2004
Materials	Chromium- or electro-plated steel, white or black polyethylene terephtalate (PET) sheeting or transparent polycarbonate sheeting
Size (mm/in.)	660/26 wide, 914/36 high, 620/24⅜ deep

Källemo, located in the same town as the venerable Bruno Mathsson's furniture firm, has produced some unorthodox furniture, such as seating by Mats Theselius. Its more traditional seating has included a reproduction of Erik Chambert's side chair from the 1930 Stockholmsufställningen (Stockholm exhibition).

The seating surface of its Flex Stacking Chair is a highly simple response to upholstery. A single plastic sheet, pierced in four corners, slips over a metal frame.

The designer is the son of a carpenter in the small Icelandic village of Akureyri. His experiences with form

and materials began with this relationship.

About his approach, he explains: "There is nothing new under the sun, but there can always be a new understanding of well-known objects. The chair, for instance, is an example of this.

"The process of designing furniture that can be made without screws or glue is a very good exercise in exploring the essence of the construction....

"You must have full control because the harmony between form and structure must be total.... [Yet] design is more than just working with forms."

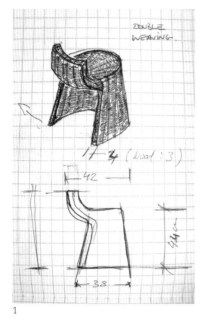

1. One of the designer's sketches which indicates "DOUBLE WEAVING." The dimensions of the final version are different.

2. The elements (25 mm/ 1 in. dia.) of the rattan core that look like bamboo are screw-assembled.

3. A weaver completes the seating surface with rattan "Pitrit" fiber (3 mm/⅛ in dia.).

4. Weaving of the base section is begun.

5. Underside view with the weaver's tools.

JalanJalan Stacking Chair/Stool

Designer	Mark Gutjahr (German, b. 1973)
Manufacturer	Mande, Jakarta, Indonesia
Date of design	2003
Materials	Rattan core and rattan "Pitrit" over-weaving
Size (mm/in.)	560/22⅟₁₆ wide, 580/22¹³⁄₁₆ high, 520/20½ deep, 450/17¾ seat height

Clients served by Cologne designer Gutjahr have included Abet Laminati, Edra, Hidden, Osram, Swarovski Optik, and Swatch. He has collaborated with another, Mande, an Indonesian company, to explore wickerwork.

When asked why he chose to work with a firm in Asia, he replied: "Of course there are basketmakers in Germany. However, there are hardly any who still master the refinements of traditional craftspeople." The relationship also presented him with a welcomed opportunity to make a trip to Indonesia.

The JalanJalan may be exceptional in that Southeast

Photos: Mark Gutjahr (p. 92); Johannes Haas, Cologne (p. 93)

Asian manufacturers seldom work with accomplished professional designers. (Chekerdjian's Seating Unit is made by the same manufacturer; see pp. 40–41.)

Gutjahr provides a further insight into his chair/stool: "JalanJalan was designed [to answer the] need for a stackable stool with optimal support for the back. The material's limits were explored by using angles and curves with maximum/minimum diameters to achieve the best possible stability.

"Traditional weaving techniques are combined with a contemporary look, giving strength to the design."

1

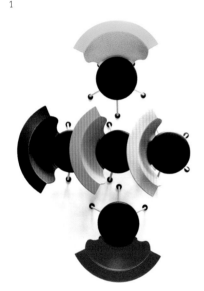

2

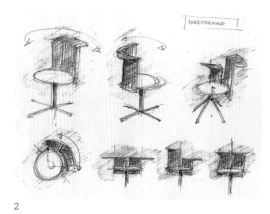

3

4

5

6

1–3. Drawings of some of the designer's first ideas.

4. The backrest material is a sheet-molded compound (SMC) composed of polypropylene and polyester fibers fused under high heat (150°C./302°F.) and high pressure. Colors available are yellow, blue, green, gray, red, or, not shown, orange, anthracite, and lime green.

5. The backrest can be fitted with a flat cushion or fully covered, front and back, in fabric or leather. The seating unit rotates 360° while the base remains stationary.

6. The base and swivel joint are polished or coated aluminum.

Turn Around Office Armchair

Designer	Udo Hasenbein (German, b. 1957)
Manufacturer	Sedus Stoll A.G., Waldshut, Germany
Date of design	2000
Materials	Polished or coated cast aluminum, polypropylene-and-polyester, fabric, or leather upholstery
Size (mm./in.)	740/29⅛ wide, 810/31⅞ high, 700/27⁹⁄₁₆ deep, 430/15¹⁵⁄₁₆ seat height

Designer and musician Hasenbein works in a studio in Haan, Germany, with Lydia Drontmann. He studied interior architecture at the Fachhochschule in Düsseldorf.

The evident whimsicality of the Turn Around Office Armchair may overshadow its use of a high-tech material for the backrest, which is formed by sophisticated sheet-molding-compound (SMC) technology. However, whimsy is generally becoming more prevalent in the design of furniture intended for the office.

The chair's main feature is its fully rotating seat over a base that remains fixed to allow for flexibility and freedom.

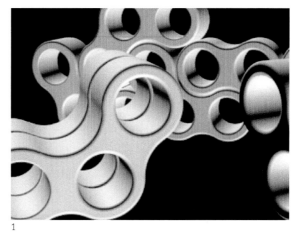

1

2

3

4

5

1. A drawing with the appearance of a molecular growth illustrates how a single form will fit into a multiple geometrical pattern.

2–3. A precise piece of machined plywood is placed over the mold after the hard-cell foam (methane diphenyl iso-cyanate—MDI) expands to form the core. (Vats holding the material to be foamed up appear in the cages in the background.) After the foam cures or becomes firm, the plywood is strongly held by the foam. And the flange, attached to rods, at the bottom of the mold pushes the object out.

4–5. Finished chairs, covered over with soft freon-free foam (20 mm/ ¾ in. thick), are shown before the upholstery fabric is fitted on.

Round One Lounge Chair

Designer	Leif Jørgensen (Danish)
Manufacturer	Hay, Horsens, Denmark
Date of design	2003
Materials	Methane diphenyl isocyanate—MDI (hard-cell foam)—and freon-free foam
Size (mm/in.)	680/26¾ wide, 340/13⅜ or 740/29⅛ high, 1000/39⅜ deep

Rolf Hay founded his eponymous firm three years ago in collaboration with clothing-and-design company Bestseller. Hay's seating is distinctive but comfortable.

The Round One Lounge Chair, part of the Round One Collection, was designed by Leif Jørgensen, whose Loop Arkitekt studio is located in Dragør, Denmark. The pieces in the collection, two chairs and a chaise, are both mono-lithic and hollow.

Some observers have noted that it recalls Joe Colombo's 1969 Tube Chair. However, the latter used no advanced technology and comprises three completely separate tubes.

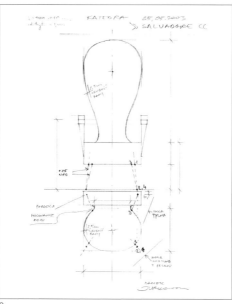

1. A developmental sketch.

2. One of the technical drawings of the high-back armchair.

3. Back view of a beech-wood high-back armchair before the surface is gold-leafed.

4. Traditional gold leaf is applied as a matte finish on frame and legs and polished around the edge of the seat.

5. A gold-leafed chair with the upholstery lining.

6. Chairs are upholstered in red Alcantara, a hard-wearing suedelike material (68% polyester and 30% polyurethane). Versions of the chairs were installed (with a lectern) in the neo-baroque cathedral in Kielce, Bazylika Katedralna Wniebowzięcia Najświętszej Marii Panny (Cathedral Basilica of the Assumption of the Blessed Virgin Mary). Some of the chairs and a lectern are shown here *in situ*.

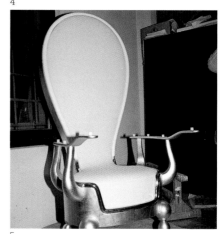

Salvadore Side Chair and Armchair

Designer	Maciek Jurkowski (Polish, b. 1969)
Manufacturer	Maciek Jurkowski Design, Katowice, Poland
Date of design	2004
Materials	Beechwood, gold leaf, Alcantara fabric
Size (mm/in.)	Side chair: 500/19^{11}⁄₁₆ wide, 970/38^{3}⁄₁₆ high, 600/23^{5}⁄₈ deep

Jurkowski, whose work is normally more contemporary in appearance, had the idea of using gold leaf on furniture after visiting the workshop of a friend who restored old picture frames. While in Moscow, he was also impressed by the use of gold in objects and historic interiors there.

For the Salvadore seating range he studied 17th- and 18th-century chairs and combined their aesthetic with that of Salvador Dalí, after whom the series is named.

He chose Alcantara, made in Italy, as an upholstery material due to its durability and soil-resistance.

Some time after producing the chair, he received a

commission to equip the cathedral in Kielce, a town in southeastern Poland. After inspecting the altar there, he realized that the Salvadore design might provide the basis for an appropriate solution.

For the church, he adapted the front of the seat slightly and other elements for ecclesiastic use.

He made the suite for the cathedral himself. A high-back version was built for the archbishop, smaller versions for bishops, side chairs for priests, and stools for their assistants. The use or commissioning of new furniture for such a setting is probably unusual.

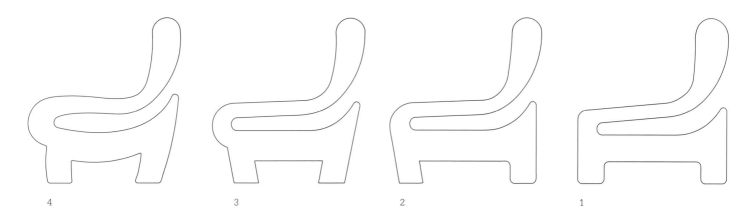

4   3   2   1

1–4. The designer's elevation drawings show the evolution of the silhouette.

5. Two chairs are cut out with a saw (not with a hot wire) from a block of four glued layers of polyurethane foam (33 kg/m, 100 mm/3¹⁵⁄₁₆ in. thick). The layers can be seen in the photograph on the facing page.

6. An ironic juxtaposition —the designer's shoes reflect the springy nature of the seat.

7. Digital images of the chair, accompanied by design instructions as CAD renderings, were transmitted to the manufacturer via the Internet.

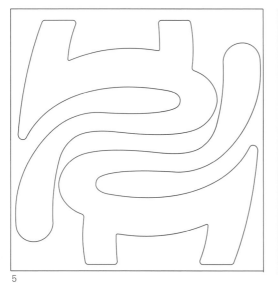

5

6

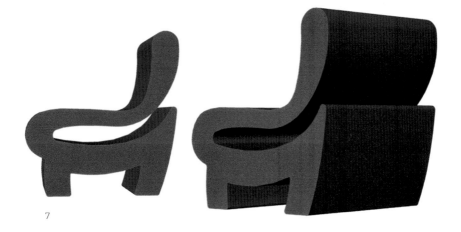

7

Twirl Lounge Chair

Designer	Ronen Kadushin (Israeli, b. 1964)
Manufacturer	Golmat Ltd., Kibbutz Yakum, Israel
Date of design	2002–04
Materials	Closed-cell polyurethane foam (33 kg/m)
Size (mm/in.)	400/15¾ wide, 820/32¼ high, 800/31½ deep

Kadushin studied at Jerusalem's Bezalel Academy, where he subsequently taught, as well as at other institutions in Israel. He became a partner in furniture- and industrial-design firm D>W (Design to Work Ltd.) in Tel Aviv. He recently settled in Berlin.

His Twirl Lounge Chair, the second item in the Oneliners collection, is unusual due to the absence of direct designer contact with the manufacturer.

The chair, in the designer's words, explores "the possibilities of design with computer-controlling… using the Internet as a communications medium.

"A two-dimensional 'cut-out' line of the chair was drawn [by me] with CAD software and sent via email to the producer, who cut out the chair from a block of foam with a CNC foam-cutting machine directly from [my] file.

"Since the foam-cutting machine is essentially a precise band saw, the saw blade must enter the foam block, cut out the desired pattern, and exit the block. This presented a design challenge: no isolated holes [should exist], and the product [was to be cut out in] one continuous line. Hence, the collection's title: Oneliners.

"The outcome is a complete product, with no finishing or assembly needed," Kadushin adds.

Concerning the absence of in-person designer/ manufacturer contact, he says, "Even at the time [of the chair's being made], the guys at the company didn't let me know when the actual production was taking place....

"What is important to me is the fact that a design was sent as email for direct manufacturing—no tooling, no molds—and, in the end, there's a complete product that is repeatable and modifiable. This gives me independence to design exactly what I want. And what I want is the freedom to express myself as a designer."

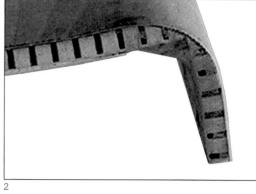

1. The three elements of seat, backrest, and backrest support are hand-layered, molded, and lacquered plywood, composed of grooved MDF, laminated on both sides with ultra-flexible 2 mm/¹⁄₁₆ in. plywood (13 mm/½ in. total thickness). Layers are adhered with an epoxy-resin glue.

(Elements are to be normal plywood or fiberglass in the final multiple production.)

2. The undercurve of the plywood seat for the all-wood prototype is notched to accommodate bending.

3. The aluminum sections—legs and

spacers—are 12 mm/½ in. thick and attached with screws. (Legs are to be chromium-plated steel tubing in the final multiple production.) The black vulcanized mold-formed gaskets of the screw connectors are ethylene propylene diene monomer (EPDM).

4. All-wood prototype.

Shell Stacking Side Chair

Designer	Beat Karrer (Swiss, b. 1966)
Manufacturer	Prototype
Date of design	2003
Materials	Aluminum, hand-laminated plywood, medium-density fiberboard (MDF)
Size (mm/in.)	400/15¾ wide, 840/33¹⁄₁₆ high, 500/19¹¹⁄₁₆ deep

Karrer studied the theory of carpentry at the Gestalterische Berufsmittelschule (college of design) in Zürich. Since 2000, he has served a number of prominent clients and has designed interiors and exhibitions.

The fundamental objective of the Shell Stacking Side Chair, composed of only nine elements, was to design a single "shell" that would comprise all the basic elements, excluding the legs.

Further illuminating the concept, Karrer offers: "The basic idea of the Shell is to get three components out of one form. Following that concept, the seat, backrest,

Photos: Beat Karrer (p. 102); Luca Zanier (p. 103)

and support are produced out of one and the same form. [Thus, there is] no wasted material. This reduction makes the production process enormously cost-effective and, additionally, gives the chair a clear and logical appearance.

'The result is a stackable chair that can be connected to a row of seats, packed compactly, and assembled very easily.

"It is composed of the classical chair components, produced with modern techniques, and has a contemporary look."

1 Geza: gabon wood, metal

2 Klipa Gdola: plywood, stainless steel

3 Bagav: polypropylene

4 Takua I: gabon wood, metal

5 Cholev: pearwood

Kaufman Seats

Designer	Yaacov Kaufman (Russian/Polish/Israeli, b. 1945)
Manufacturer	Unique examples
Date of design	2000
Materials	Various
Size (mm/in.)	Various

Born in Russia, Kaufman lived in Poland until 1957 when he emigrated to Israel. Today he lives and works in Tel Aviv/Jaffa and also works in Jerusalem and Milan.

Highly accomplished, he has received a number of prestigious prizes and been granted many international patents in the fields of lamp-arm motion structures, furniture, exhibitions, the ergonomics of seating, and others.

His practice as both an industrial designer and an artist can be seen in the chairs and stools considered here, all conceived and made within a short time.

His theories about stools and chairs include: "The

6 Nekudot: steel, rubber, aluminum, leather

7 Ched: plywood, stainless steel

8 Het Hatabaat: aluminum, polyvinylchloride (PVC)

9 Klipa: plywood, string

10 Amud: pearwood, recycled carpet

11 Tlat Reik: plywood, steel

12 Takua III: gabon wood, metal

13 Prusot: stainless steel, polyvinylchloride (PVC)

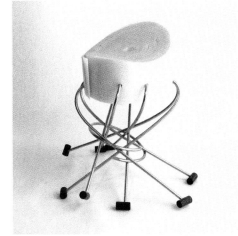
14 Zaza: polypropylene, stainless steel, rubber

stool [is] an object both dividing and connecting us to the ground. Stools are the beginning of chairs.

"The trunk [of a tree] was probably one of the primary elements in the evolution of stools.

"This group [of stools and chairs shown here] is a way of looking back into the evolution of the stool from the trunk, to later become a chair.

"These various formations of stools can be used as a checklist for questioning: Were there other evolutionary forms and roads taken? Is there a moment between a stool and a chair?"

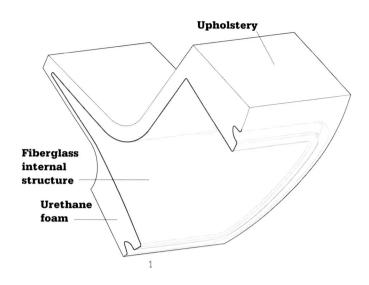

Upholstery

Fiberglass internal structure

Urethane foam

1

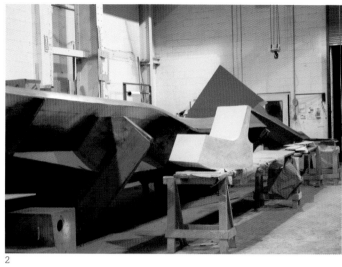

2

1. The polyester resin-impregnated fiberglass internal structure with integral rails is over-molded with urethane foam. The hollow interior reduces the amount of foam normally required in solid-foam seating.

2. A chair body before the upholstery sleeve is pulled over the foam.

3. The curved bottom edge of the fiberglass shell offers a hard rocking edge.

4. Almost any fabric for the upholstery is acceptable.

3

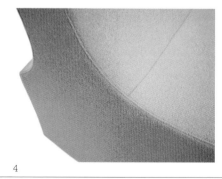

4

Toc Lounge Chair

Designer	Scot Laughton (Canadian, b. 1962)
Manufacturer	Lolah Inc., Mississauga, Ontario, Canada
Date of design	2002
Materials	Fiberglass/polyester resin, molded urethane foam, fabric
Size (mm/in.)	Lounge chair: 610/24 wide, 787/31 high, 813/32 deep; settee: 914/36 wide with same height and depth

A former student of industrial design and subsequently a teacher in Toronto, Laughton established the manufacturer Portico with two partners. Its first product was a lamp that he had designed in his design-student days.

In 1992, he set up his own studio to serve Canadian firms such as the newly established Lolah, of which Laughton is the design director.

His work has drawn a number of awards and is included in the collections of the Royal Ontario Museum and Toronto's DX. He was elected the 2003 Designer of the Year by the Interior Design Show committee in Toronto.

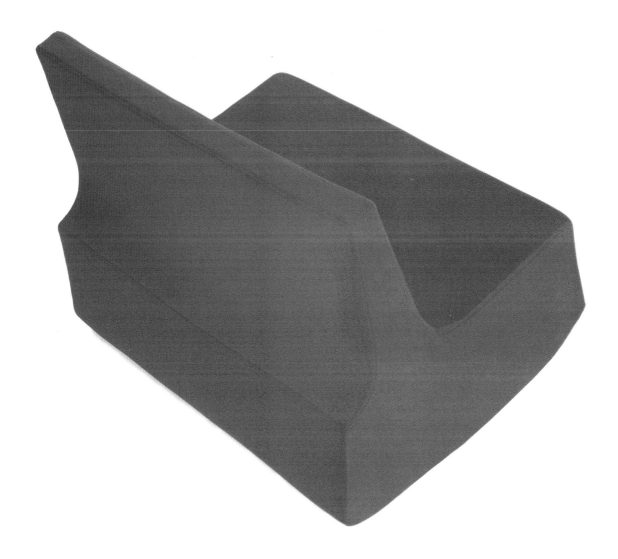

About his rocker's genesis, he says: "The idea for Toc started with the idea to update the family [or traditional] rocking chair. It was designed as a single form with the rails of the rocker integral with the fiberglass support body [that is] captured within the upholstered urethane foam. The Toc takes advantage of the boat-construction technology [for yacht furniture] at Lolah's parent company, where fiberglass and fabrics are used.

"The fiberglass body supports the foam, reduces the the amount of foam [normally required], provides rocking rails, and offers a detail for securing the upholstery."

1

2

1–2. Initial experimental models were composed of coat hangers, without the hook, to make "an icon of a stool" and "symbols of legs," according to the designer. Double coat hangers strengthen the legs, and all are held in place with locking plastic pull-fasteners.

3–4. A subsequent stage was again constructed of coat hangers. The sections are welded together.

3

4

Spring Chair

Designer	Raviv Lifshitz (Israeli, b. 1968)
Manufacturer	The designer
Date of design	2002–03
Materials	Chromium-plated or painted steel rods and polyvinylchloride (PVC) film
Size (mm/in.)	450/17¹¹⁄₁₆ wide, 750/29½ high, 500/19¹¹⁄₁₆ deep

Like a number of professional designers in Israel, Lifshitz is a graduate of the Bezalel Academy in Jerusalem.

In addition to having worked at several firms, he has pursued the development of theoretical ideas. Lifshitz may be best known for reprocessing anonymous designs—or readymades—for new uses, such as turning the skeletal frames of umbrellas into lighting fixtures and PVC pipes into shoes. Likewise, the structures leading to his Pumpkin Stool (see page 110) and Spring Chair were composed of wire coat-hanger elements. However, Lifshitz abandoned the use of coat-hanger wire in favor of his own production

techniques and the manipulation of raw materials.

About the Spring Chair he explains: "The concept
underlying its invention is the cage [that can house]
inflatable forms to create various functional structures
and products (chairs, stools, lamp shades, screens, etc.).
[Proper function] depends on the shape of the element,
the spatial and physical interactions, and various
supporting sections."

Lifshitz's objective was realized through extensive
experimentation with steel-rod construction and a search
for a suitable high-pressure inflation bag.

Experiments follow >

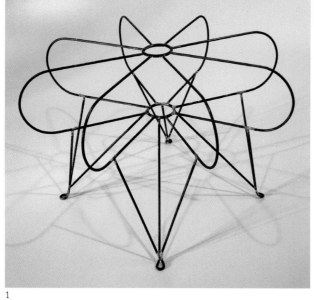

1

2

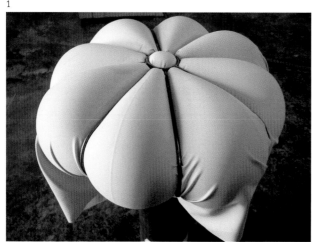

3

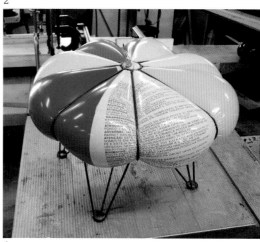

4

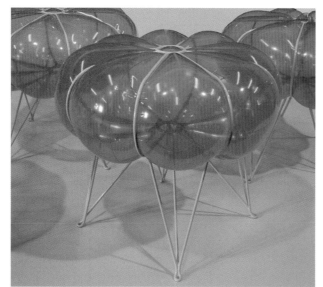

5

1–2. Graduating from the use of coat hangers, the basic structure of the eight-part top portion and three-stemmed legs was developed.

3–4. Further experiments were conducted with latex sheeting (3) and an industrial balloon (4).

5. Ultimately, Lifshitz's Pumpkin Stools with orange transparent balloons feature PVC-coated frames. The frame of his Bride's Seat, a white stool (not shown here), is also PVC-coated.

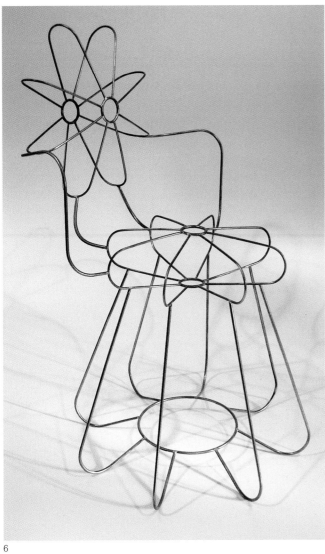

6

7

8

6. A base entirely different from the stool's was developed for the Spring Chair with printed transparent balloons inflated within the backrest and seat cages.

7. The structure is silver-welded and PVC-coated.

8. The inflation valve protrudes within the ring of the backrest.

1 2 3

4 5 6

1–6. The six sequential images illustrate the transformation.

7. Even though the wheels on the ends of the legs are not shown here, the drawing includes the elements of the mechanism.

8. The arrows in this drawing, including the wheels, show that the arms are to be pulled out and down, that the cushion with feet is to be removed and placed on the floor, and that the back is to be pulled forward and down. The chair's wood frame is layered with polyester padding over polyurethane foam. The foam and padding were specifically developed to meet the demands of this chair/bed. The upholstery is removable.

9. Nylon wheels rotate within the tubular-steel legs.

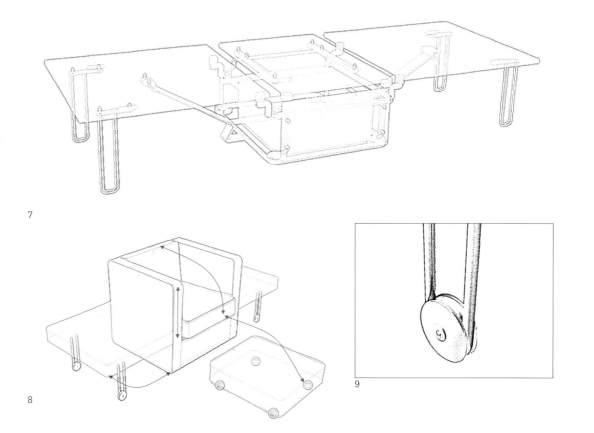

7

8

9

Acca Club Chair/Bed

Designer	Giulio Manzoni (Italian, b. 1952)
Manufacturer	Campeggi S.r.l., Anzano del Parco (CO), Italy
Date of design	2003
Materials	Tubular steel, acrylonitrate butadiene styrene (ABS), polyurethane foam, polyester padding, multi-layered wood, nylon wheels, fabric
Size (mm./in.)	Chair: 830/32¹¹⁄₁₆ wide, 750/29½ high, 750/29½ deep; bed: 2040/80⁵⁄₁₆ wide, 400/15¾ high, 750/29½ deep

Architect/designer Manzoni is active in Cremona, Italy. He has collaborated with Paola Navone and others.

He designed this club chair/bed for Campeggi, a firm that has become known for its often-unusual convertible furniture specially conceived to serve today's small domiciles.

Ottomans that can be made into beds and sofa/beds are, of course, a familiar concept. However, Manzoni's chair/bed is different in that it is also very comfortable.

The manufacturer emphasizes that the Acca is "a new type of convertible armchair, chaise longue, and single

Photos: Ph. Ezio Prandini

bed. The Acca, through very simple movements, adapts itself to various needs, very easily, and can be moved from one room to another. [Its mobility is facilitated] thanks to its wheels and its small dimensions which allow its being pushed through a standard doorway."

When the cushion, fitted with feet and usable as a kind of bedside table, is removed, the area beneath will hold bed linen and other items.

When the arms and back are pushed down, the efficient mechanical structure transforms the chair into its lounging or sleeping position.

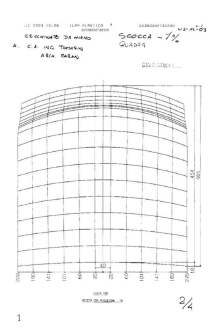

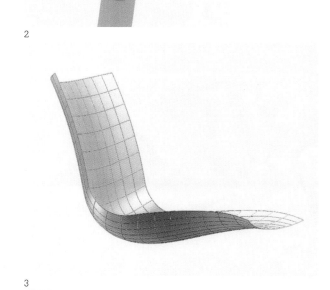

1

2

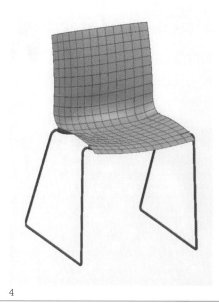

4

3

5

1. The mesh placement (in plan view here) is precisely configured.

2. A computer image of the underside connector of the legs to the shell on the straight-leg model.

3–4. Computer studies.

5. The shell is a bi-injection-molded combination of GE's Lexan® clear polycarbonate with a mesh of Bayer's mass-colored Desmopan® aliphatic thermoplastic polyurethane (TPU). The TPU composite is ordinarily used to make toothbrush handles and cellular-phone cases.

With and without arms, stackable versions are available with a slide base (shown) or with four legs; there is also a version with a center base.

X3 Side Chair

Designer	Marco Maran (Italian, b. 1963)
Manufacturer	Maxdesign S.r.l., Bagnaria Arsa (UD), Italy
Date of design	2003
Materials	Bi-injection-molded Lexan® polycarbonate/Desmopan®, chromium-plated steel rod or tubular stainless steel
Size (mm/in.)	500/20 wide, 760/29^{15}/₁₆ high, 470/18½ deep

Maran studied art in his hometown of Siena and attended the Università degli Studi in Florence. He has received prizes for his chairs, apparently a specialty.

The seating shell of the X3 is more about technology than aesthetics. It is produced by the bi-injection molding of a clear polycarbonate with a colored mesh grid that is an aliphatic thermoplastic polyurethane. Extensive technological and ergonomic studies were conducted to produce this lightweight, comfortable, and robust element.

The process, which applies this complex molding technology to seating for the first time, has been patented.

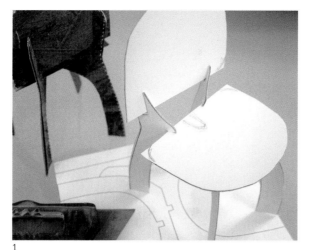

1

1. Developmental maquettes in various materials, originally but not ultimately notch-fitted in this manner.

2. A chair, here as a prototype, is composed of four parts to be screwed together. To economize on the material by eliminating wastage, the backrest and seat are taken from the space between the legs.

Facing page: Notice that there is a notch in the top edge of the one of the seat supports and in the bottom edge of the other. Thus, one part slides over the other to form the superstructure (see the red circle in image 2). The backrest and seat are screwed on.

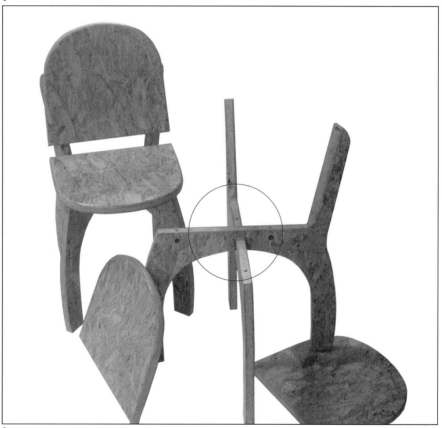

2

Tangram Side Chair

Designers	Nó Design (Flavio Barão Di Samo, b. 1978; Léonardo Massarelli, b. 1970; and Marcio Giannelli, b. 1977), Brazilian
Manufacturer	BFC Brazilian Furniture Connection, Miami, Florida, US
Date of design	2004
Materials	Oriented strand board (OSB) and screws
Size (mm/in.)	Assembled: 450/17¾ wide, 880/34⅝ high, 500/19¹¹⁄₁₆ deep; flat: 630/24¹³⁄₁₆ wide, 930/36⅝ high, 20/¾ thick

The Brazilian design team frequently begin by considering the materials to be recycled for their tabletop items and home-furnishing designs. Examples include Runned Over Bowls made from old vehicle tires and the Moth Chair made from shopping bags.

The Nó group's objective for the Tangram was to develop an ecologically respectful, inexpensive chair. Its parts are fitted together, like the Chinese puzzle of the same name, to optimize the use of the material. The material they chose—oriented strand board—is cheap and strong and composed of the fibers of only small, fast-growing trees.

Rough sketches and production follow >

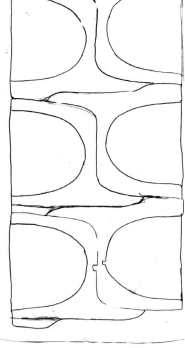

1

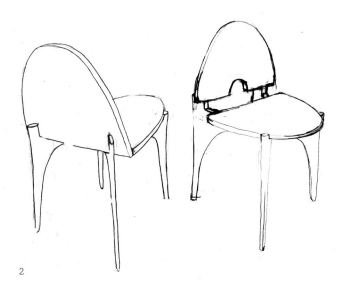

2

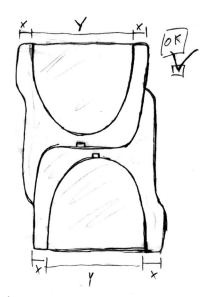

3

4

5. Oriented strand board (OSB) that evolved from waferboard was introduced in 1978. It has essentially replaced plywood in some countries. OSB is unique in that long wood strands are specifically, not randomly, oriented in layered mats. The strands are up to 150 mm/ 5⅞ in. long and 25 mm/ 1 in. wide. The OSB sheet for the Tangram Chair is 20 mm/¾ in. thick.

1–2. As well as maquettes, sketches were rendered in order to arrive at the best form to utilize most of the area of a single piece of board.

3–4. The parts in these rather loose sketches are arranged, much like a puzzle, in a manner to eliminate waste by maximizing the number of parts possible from a standard board size. Thus, the design, or shape, of the chair is beholden to the configuration.

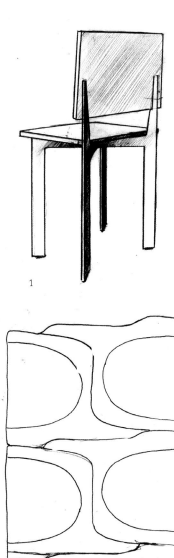

5

6

6.–7. A computer-numeric-controlled (CNC) saw cuts the four parts of a single chair from one piece of board. (The backrest and seat parts have been removed in image 7.)

8. The edges are rounded with an electric sander to eliminate roughness.

9. The five finished parts are fitted together, same as when sawed out, and make for a thin in-box profile. Instructions for assembly are printed on the packing box which also contains the necessary screws for the attachment of the back and seat.

7

8

9

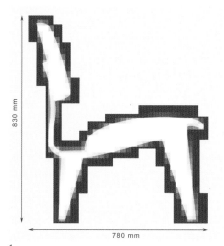

1

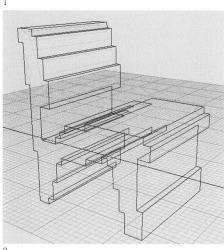

2

1. A side view shows three qualities of resolution.

2. A three-dimensional image of the foam extrusion form was drawn using a computer CAD program.

3–4. The substructure, backrest, and seat are 3 or 4 mm/⅛ or ³⁄₁₆ in. sheet metal that has been formed and bent by computer-numeric-controlled (CNC) machinery. The vertical struts afford extra support. The joints are carbon dioxide (CO_2) welded, which is welding with consumable electrodes in an atmosphere of CO_2 gas.

5. Twelve or so sections of soft polyurethane foam are adhered to the superstructure as horizontal planes in contrast to the curves of the hollow superstructure. And the backrest and seat are thus camouflaged.

Facing page: The surface of the polyurethane is flock-fiber-coated to achieve a velveteen-like touch.

3

4

5

Lo-Res Lounge Chair

Designer	Guido Ooms (Dutch, b. 1974)
Manufacturers	Instaal, Eindoven; Racticel Holding B.V.; and Flock Techniek Nederland; all Netherlands
Date of design	2002
Materials	Sheet metal, polyurethane foam, flocking
Size (mm/in.)	550/21⅝ wide, 830/32¹¹⁄₁₆ high, 780/30¹¹⁄₁₆ deep

A graduate of the Design Academy in Eindhoven, Ooms works both alone and with others, and, not unlike many young Dutch designers today, produces highly eccentric work. Unconventional pieces include a human-hair hat and, with Davy Grosemans, sex toys in porcelain purporting to be alternatives to kitsch windmill-, clog-, cow-, and tulip-image ceramic souvenirs.

His Lo-Res Lounge Chair is a bit more orthodox, but not much. About his use of computer technology and CNC-directed machinery for its realization, Ooms laments: "The digital world often forces trade-offs between two

opposing preferences: speed and quality.

"When working with images, speed often translates to lower resolution, compressing elements into simplified shapes. During this process, it is the computer, compelled by necessity, that makes the decisions about what is taken out and what is left. If we apply this bargain to existing products, we see that certain aspects of the product come to the front while others recede."

Nevertheless, the Lo-Res Lounge Chair is hardly an anonymous design. Its distinctive aspects were determined by Oooms's choices of the "computer decisions."

1

2

3

4

5

1–2. The wholly hand-crafted lounge chair in rattan begins, of course, with the frame.

3–4. Rows of contiguous rattan rods are nailed onto and around the frame.

5. A craftsperson measures the overhang of the ends.

6. An opening outlined with a rattan ring permits easier moving when the chaise is placed on its side with your hand in the hole for lifting.

7. The opening at the end is filled in with short rattan stalks which have the appearance of wooden dowels. This filler in the front end gives the impression that the chaise is completely filled with rattan stalks. The chaise is actually hollow (seen in image 6); otherwise, it would be impracticably heavy. Its weight is 48 kg/106 lbs.

Rattan, a member of the palm family, is not bamboo but rather the stem of a giant tropical grass that can reach over 4 m/13 ft. tall. These vines, only found in Asia, crawl along the ground and climb onto trees to reach sunlight.

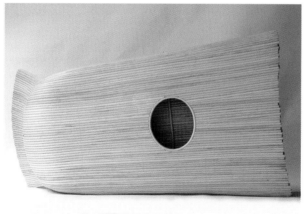

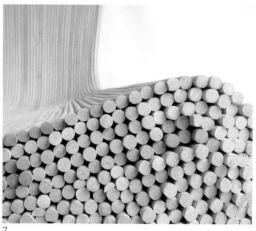

6

7

Pare Chaise Longue

Designer	Anon Pairot (Thai, b. 1979)
Manufacturer	Planet 2001 Co., Ltd., Bangkok, Thailand
Date of design	2004
Materials	Rattan and nails
Size (mm/in.)	1050/41⅜ wide, 1100/43⁵⁄₁₆ high, 2100/82¹¹⁄₁₆ deep

Pairot, a young and energetic designer living and working in Bangkok, creates furniture and furnishings that not only incorporate materials native to his country but also others such as plastics and glass.

He says his Pare Chaise Longue, in area-indigenous rattan, is an expression of "tropical minimalist thought."

He adds: "The concept aims to reduce waste through a simple and effective design [hollow inside but appearing otherwise] and was inspired by the traditional bamboo rafts that Thai people call *pare*. These strongly structured boats hold the heavy weight of almost any type of cargo."

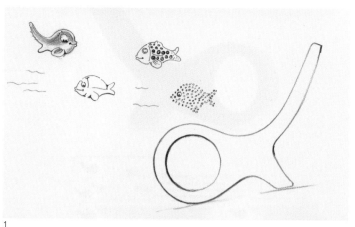

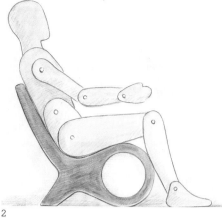

1

2

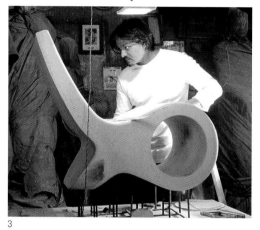

3

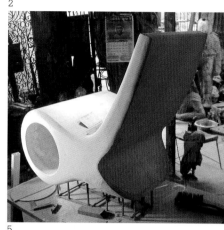

4

5

6

7

1–2. The idea began with sketches on paper and with a computer, including ergonomic studies.

3. A plaster model was cast to determine the desired profile. A welded-steel stand, composed of a number of rods, was built to support the plaster model and aid the sculpting.

4. Another steel support structure was built, and the model inverted for access to the underside.

5. The model was then set upright again for sanding and other final finishing.

6. A fiberglass-and-resin mold was made from the plaster model.

7. A fiberglass-mold section forms a final chair in Du Pont's Corian®. In the last stage of production, a special satin-finish coating creates ivory or pearl effects.

Though the designer has a studio in Amsterdam, this work was carried out in India.

Fish Lounge Chair

Designer	Satyendra Pakhalé (Indian, b. 1967)
Manufacturer	Cappellini S.p.A., Arosio (CO), Italy
Date of design	2002
Materials	Corian®
Size (mm/in.)	550/21⅝ wide, 740/29⅛ high, 810/31⅞ deep, 400/15¾ seat height

Active in a studio in the Netherlands and a workshop in his native India, Satyendra Pakhalé attends to a long list of high-design clients, and his range of products and vehicles is likewise extensive. He refers to himself as a "cultural nomad" and qualifies for the title on the grounds of his extensive travels.

Some observers have noted that he works like a sculptor and behaves like an architect, which perhaps implies both that his work has a sculptural quality and that his pursuit of its fulfillment is fastidious. The Fish Lounge Chair may well serve as an archetype of his approach.

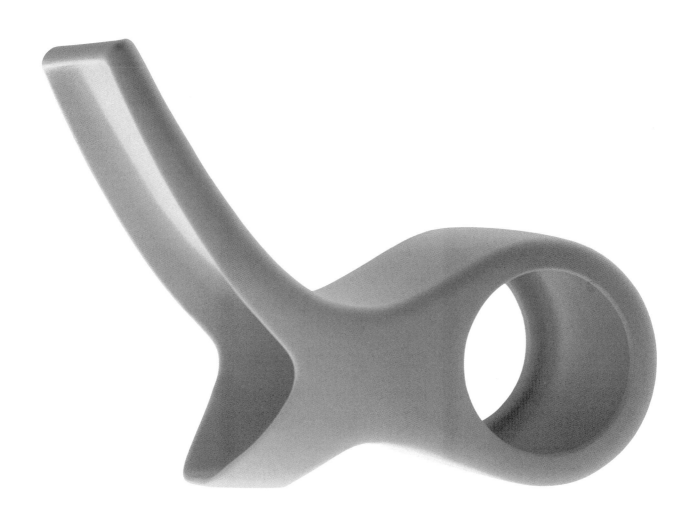

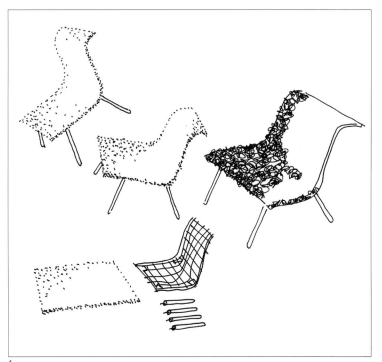

1. Some of the designer's sketches.

2. A close view of the tough Nomad™ matting by the 3M company in the US reveals its curly nature. Two sheets are placed over the chair's frame. The material is intended to be used as a carpet for shoe scraping at the entry of an interior space to eliminate dirt and moisture from being tracked into a room. It can be cleaned by shaking, vacuuming, or washing with a hose.

3. The frame, painted silver, is a welded structure of sheet metal and 5 mm/³⁄₁₆ in. dia. steel wire to form a 52 x 52 mm/2 x 2 in. grid.

4. The detachable stainless-steel tubular legs (30 mm/1³⁄₁₆ in. dia.) include threaded pins at the tops (not shown) and rounded-foot sections.

The Rubber Chair

Designer	Jiři Pelcl (Czech, b. 1950)
Manufacturer	Atelier Pelcl, Prague, Czech Republic
Date of design	2004
Materials	Sheet steel, steel wire, stainless-steel tubing, Nomad™ vinyl-fiber matting by 3M
Size (mm/in.)	650/25⅝ wide, 650/25⅝ high, 700/27⁹⁄₁₆ deep

Pelcl studied architecture at the Vysoká Škola Umelecko-průmyslová in Prague and furniture design at London's Royal College of Art. In 1987, he cofounded Atika, a Czech avant-garde group with an approach much like that of the Anti-Design movement in Italy. Since 2002, he has headed the school where he studied architecture.

In the Rubber Chair, the use of the matting—actually a shoe-scraping carpet—is unusual. Pelcl chose the material for its high-performance characteristics and distinctive appearance. Two thin layers over a wire grid offer comfort and foster a slim silhouette.

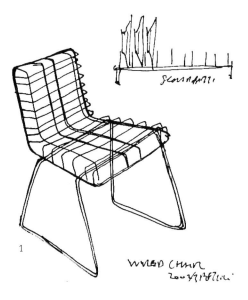

1

2

3

4

5

6

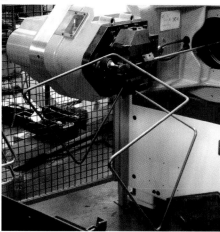

7

1. In the upper-right corner of one of the designer's sketches, a standard wire rack for drying dishes is shown. It is produced by the same process as that for Pezzini's side chair.

2. The steel rods reach the manufacturer in the form of wound bales.

3. Each intersection of the wires is spot-electrowelded by computer-directed machinery.

4. After the seat structure is welded, it is bent into shape.

5–6. The leg support is also bent by computer-controlled machinery for precision.

7. Chairs are available chromium-plated or, for outdoor use, epoxy powder-coated. Four plastic glides (not shown) can be snapped onto the horizontal leg slides for floor protection. Seat pads are available.

Wired Stacking Chair

Designer	Gabriele Pezzini (Italian, b. 1963)
Manufacturer	Maxdesign S.r.l., Bagnaria Arsa (UD), Italy
Date of design	2003
Materials	Wire
Size (mm/in.)	500/19¹¹⁄₁₆ wide, 790/31⅛ high, 550/21⅝ deep

Having studied photography and then industrial design at the ISIA in Florence, Pezzini now works in Milan. Highly active, he has designed a number of imaginative products, ranging from furniture to bathroom fittings.

For his Wired Chair, he looked to the inexpensive products being produced by electrowelding wire, like CD holders and dish-drying racks. Production of a chair in wire must necessarily be reliant upon the technology that a manufacturer either already has in place or is willing to install. Pezzini's solution, which permits stackability and includes a flex for comfort, satisfies the demands of production.

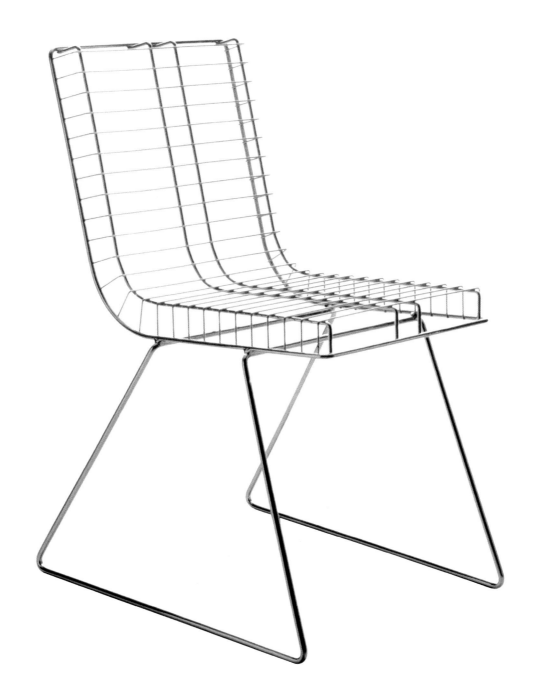

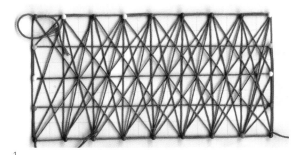

1

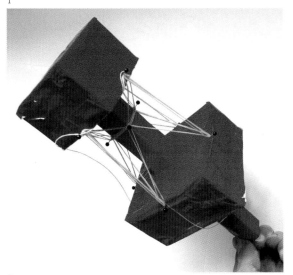

2

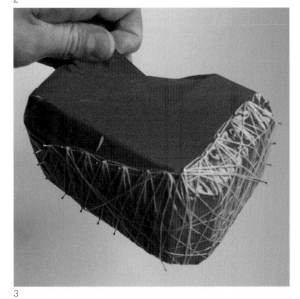

3

1. The weave pattern of the seat was first investigated using colored string.

2–3. The base (2) and seat shell (3) were likewise string-developed at a small scale. The seat shell (shown over a mold) and base are woven or built of carbon fiber which is ultimately epoxy-coated and heated.

4. Chairs are made in a factory whose specialty is woven rattan. For strength and desirable aesthetics, the chair's construction is thicker and stronger in some areas and lighter and more transparent in others. To serve different structural needs, the seat and supporting structure are made separately.

The weight of a chair is 1.5 kg/3³⁄₁₆ lbs.

Production marries a high-tech material with low-tech craftsmanship.

4

Carbon Side Chair

Designers	Bertjan Pot (Dutch, b. 1975) and Marcel Wanders (Dutch, b. 1963)
Manufacturer	Moooi B.V., Breda, Netherlands
Date of design	2004
Materials	Carbon fiber and epoxy
Size (mm/in.)	460/18⅛ wide, 750/29½ high, 500/19¹¹⁄₁₆ deep

Wanders and Pot have become known for their use of advanced materials, particularly carbon fiber. Wanders explored it in his 1995 Knotted Chair, and Pot in his 2003 Random Chair.

The prototype of Pot's Carbon Copy Chair is a replica of Charles and Ray Eames's 1950–53 Plastic Side Chair. Thus: a "carbon copy" (Pot's chair) from "carbon paper" (the Eameses' chair).

About the prototype Pot asks: "Did you ever use carbon tracing paper to get a copy of a drawing? Well, I used carbon fiber and epoxy resin to 'sketch' a 3D version (strong

enough to sit on) of one of my favorite chairs. More than 50 years after Charles Eames made his plastic chair, its design and construction still stand, even in carbon, because of his brilliant engineering job. In cooperation with Marcel Wanders and inspired by the Carbon Copy, I made the Carbon Chair. This chair is completely hand-coiled and in 100% carbon fiber and epoxy (so, no metal frame!), now in the inventory of Moooi [Wanders's firm]."

The Eames "Eiffel Tower" base on Pot's prototype was altered for the Pot/Wanders Carbon Chair to a slide-type support structure, shown above.

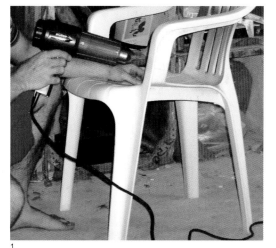

1

3

2

4

1–5. The construction by the designer is shown in production sequence.

5

The designer indicates: "A familiar picture is the stackable white chairs found in most average courtyards. I wanted to give them an identity all their own.

"When the chairs 'look at each other,' two chairs in my hands can have four legs [rather than eight] and become two 'white dogs' having a conversation.

"I removed some of what already exists in the chairs, made from polypropylene, and bent them by heat."

White Dogs Chair

Designer	Alon Razgour (Israeli, b. 1965)
Manufacturer	Unique example
Date of design	2002
Materials	Readymade plastic chairs
Size (mm/in.)	500/19¹¹⁄₁₆ wide, 1100/43⁵⁄₁₆ high, 1500/59¹⁄₁₆ deep

Razgour worked under Yaacov Kaufman (see pp. 104–05) in Italy after studying ceramics engineering, industrial design, and business. His work has included high-tech equipment, medical devices, packaging, and display units.

The White Dogs Chair is a departure for him in that it is probably more a sculpture than a chair. However, it is still a functional piece of design.

Possibly due to a scarcity of manufacturers and tradition, the manipulation of readymades—or existing products—is popular in Israel. Razgour's chair is composed of anonymous, ubiquitous outdoor chairs.

1. Some of the designer's early ideas, or doodles, were drawn on an old agenda page.

2. The chair's two sections can be rolled and held with a bungee-cord tie-down.

3–4. The designer connects the two sections with the single peripheral zipper. The removable cotton upholstery covers harmonic —or flexible—steel sheets (0.6 mm/¼₀ in. thick).

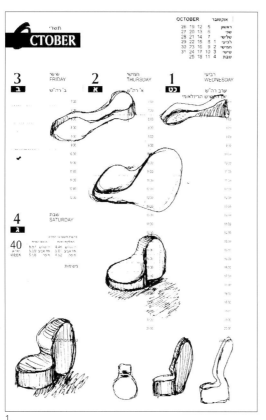

1

2

3

4

The Big Wednesday Lounge Chair

Designer	Ely Rozenberg (Israeli, b. 1969)
Manufacturer	Oz, Rome, Italy
Date of design	2002
Materials	Sheet steel, cotton fabric, a zipper
Size (mm/in.)	500/19¹¹⁄₁₆ wide, 900/35⅜ high, 600/23⅝ deep

Rozenberg, born in Dushanbe, the capital of Tajikistan, emigrated with his family to Israel at age eight. He studied industrial design at Jerusalem's Bezalel Academy.

The Big Wednesday Lounge Chair is a part of Rozenberg's Zipping Furniture series.

The seat is composed of two harmonic steel sheets and one continuous zipper. The zipper is glued along the edges of the steel sheets. The two sections are easy to assemble, move, and reassemble. The cotton surface can be removed and washed if necessary.

The chairs and other items in Rozenberg's zippered

Photos: Cinzia Camela and Sara DeBerardinis

group are, according to him, "a type of nomadic furniture that satisfies the need for comfort and serves well in today's small-space dwellings.

"The project was developed with the help of [the Japanese zipper manufacturer] Y.K.K.

"[Then] I was invited by the artist Michelangelo Pistoletto to participate in the 2003 Biennale di Venezia. The Zipping Furniture there was part of the project 'Love Difference' in 'Utopia Station.'"

Concerning the question of nomadism: "My family, like many other Jewish families, has moved from place to place. There are no two people in my family who were born in the same city. [Therefore] I became worried and preoccupied with being ready for the next move. And emigration to Israel didn't remove this primordial instinct—constantly moving from place to place.

"In the small state of Israel, people there constantly move from house to house.

"Nomadic furniture was an obvious option for a 'wandering Jew.'"

In fact, today Rozenberg has his own studio, Oz, in Rome with Alessandro Bianchini.

1   2   3

1–4. Developmental drawings arrive at shape and size. *Rinforzare* in image 1 indicates a "reinforcement" point, which ultimately appears to have been unnecessary due to the characteristics of the CSP plastic. Image 4 indicates that plastic glides are fitted onto the leg slides for floor protection (also see facing page).

5. A computer-generated back view of the voluptuous shell of the lounge-chair version.

6–7. A practice of many sophisticated furniture manufacturers is to configure a basic chair design in a range of versions as here: two stool heights, a side chair, and a lounge chair (image 5, and facing page).

Facing page: Even though this is a prototype, it is little different from the final lounge-chair version.

4   5

6   7

Maxima Lounge Chair, Side Chair, and Stools

Designer	William Sawaya (Lebanese/Italian, b. 1948)
Manufacturer	Sawaya & Moroni S.p.A., Milan, Italy
Date of design	2002
Materials	Chlorosulfonated polyurethane (CSP), stainless steel, polyurethane coating
Size (mm/in.)	660/26 wide, 762/30 high, 914/36 deep

Sawaya, who was born in Beirut, worked there initially and then in France, Italy, Japan, Greece, and the US. Almost 30 years ago he settled in Italy, where he established an architecture-and-design practice and, 12 years ago, a manufacturing facility, both with Paolo Moroni.

Sawaya designs, and also commissions from others, furniture with a strong visual presence. Michael Graves was one of the first designers to work for his firm. The list of alumni has become quite extensive.

Concerning one of his own designs, the Maxima, he says: "Remember the Jacobsen Chair? It still looks quite

contemporary [today and has maintained] its lightness,
sleekness, and simplicity through the years.

"This was [what] I had in mind for the Maxima Chair
but in a contemporary material such as compact polyurethane, combining high resistance, light flexibility, and a
folded intimate shape."

The polyurethane to which he refers is chlorosulfonated
polyurethane (CSP), an elastomer and one of a new
generation of plastics with a memory-shape characteristic:
that is, a thin profile of CSP will return to its original
shape after deformation and not split at stress points.

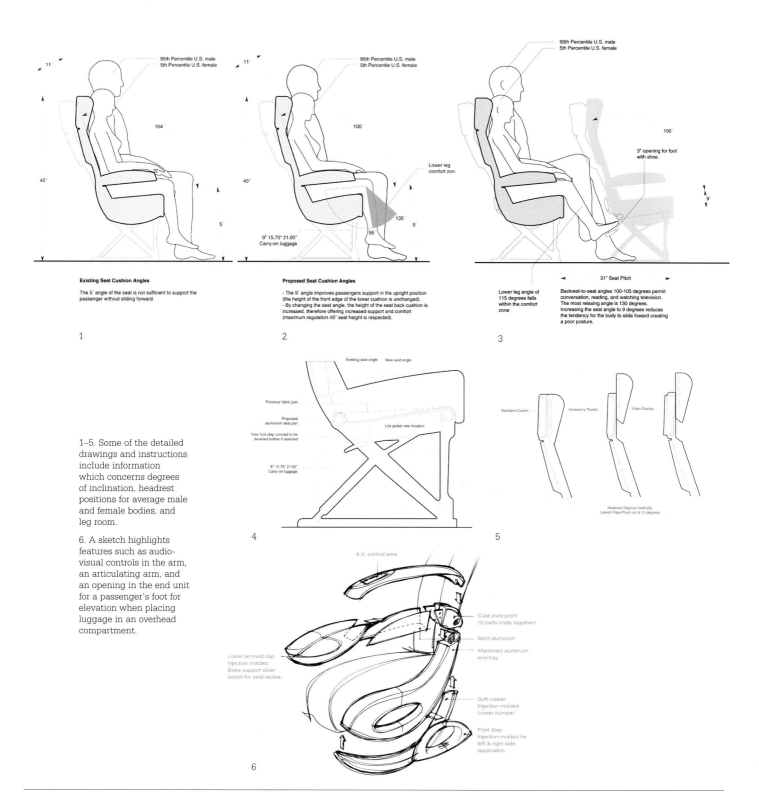

Existing Seat Cushion Angles

The 5° angle of the seat is not sufficient to support the passenger without sliding forward.

1

Proposed Seat Cushion Angles

- The 9° angle improves passengers support in the upright position (the height of the front edge of the lower cushion is unchanged).
- By changing the seat angle, the height of the seat back cushion is increased, therefore offering increased support and comfort (maximum regulation 45° seat height is respected).

2

Lower leg angle of 115 degrees falls within the comfort zone

Backrest-to-seat angles 100-105 degrees permit conversation, reading, and watching television. The most relaxing angle is 130 degrees. Increasing the seat angle to 9 degrees reduces the tendency for the body to slide foward creating a poor posture.

3

1–5. Some of the detailed drawings and instructions include information which concerns degrees of inclination, headrest positions for average male and female bodies, and leg room.

6. A sketch highlights features such as audio-visual controls in the arm, an articulating arm, and an opening in the end unit for a passenger's foot for elevation when placing luggage in an overhead compartment.

4

5

6

Weber Aircraft 5600 Tourist-Class Series

Designers	Gad Shaanan (b. 1954), François Duval (b. 1967), and Daniel Pellerin (b. 1970), Canadian; with the manufacturer's engineers: Jeff Cheung, Steven Chau, and Alexander Pozzi
Manufacturer	Weber Aircraft L.P., Gainsville, Texas, US
Date of design	2002
Materials	2024-T4 and 6061-T6 aluminum, 386 cast aluminum, 17-4 stainless steel, 4130 steel, vacuum-formed/injection-molded polycarbonate, vacuum-formed/injection-molded ABS, polyurethane foam
Size (mm/in.)	Full-up position: 1143/45 high

The designers of the Gad Shaanan Design studio worked in tandem with the manufacturer's engineers to develop this airplane chair.

Many professional designers would be incapable of designing seating to satisfy the combined specific demands of the airline industry, governmental regulations, ergonomics, and a sensitive client. All conditions must be researched (including data on average body sizes and comfort satisfaction) and tested.

There is still leeway for the inclusion of the designers' own aesthetic considerations.

The designers report: "Seat-comfort level is a major complaint of airline passengers. For airlines, it is important to be able to get as many passengers as possible into an aircraft and be able to quickly service, repair, or change the seats. The main objective [for the Weber example] was to develop a new seat that would meet both the needs of the passenger and the airline.

"The Weber 5600 Tourist-Class Series was designed with a translating, or adjustable, seat bottom that actually uses less space to accomplish a greater incline. Instead of just tilting for the recline, the new seat also incorporates an adjustable motion within the seat bottom. This new concept allows a passenger to recline to a full 17° angle, while only using 4 in. [100 mm] of back motion. The result is a more enjoyable flight because a passenger can recline farther [while leaving open the leg room behind the front seat].

"Additional features include an ergonomically contoured seat back and bottom, injection-molded armcaps, and a large underseat clearance. Optional 'first-class'-type features are a four-way adjustable headrest, PC and accessory power outlets, adjustable lumbar support, etc."

Prototypes and final configurations follow >

1

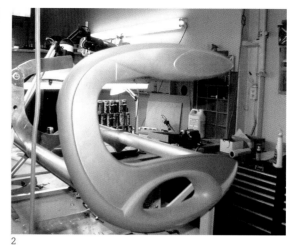

2

3

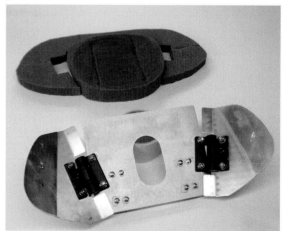

4

5

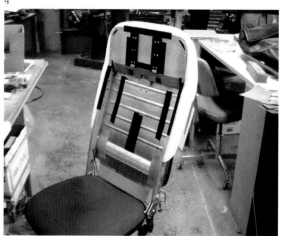

6

Facing page:

7–8. Three-seat and two-seat configurations.

Special features of the production model:
An energy-absorbing leg to reduce passenger and floor loads during severe, 16G acceleration.

A reduced number of total parts.

The easy reconfiguration and high interchange of components.

The accommodation of Matsushita Avionics, Thales Avionics, and Rockwell Collins in-flight entertainment (IFE) systems.

Diminished bottom-cushion height and a rounded bullnose edge to reduce deep-vein thrombosis (DVT).

A thin backrest and headrest for more passenger space.

A thin quick-release tray table with a scalloped bottom and a front surface for more passenger space.

A clamp-on leg and spreader.

Prototypes of elements:

1. Armrest.

2. End unit.

3. Fold-up footrest.

4. Headrest structure and foam padding.

5. Polyurethane-foam cushion.

6. Backrest and seat.

7

8

1. A dimensional drawing has notations which concern calculations, the usage of the raw steel sheet, and other comments.

2. Because the prototype in 16-gauge steel did not function properly with a single bend at the top, a special tool was devised to impress a double bend. Finally, when a chair is placed on the floor, the back slides out at the bottom from 25 to 75 mm/ 1 to 3 in.

3. A raw-steel prototype is shown. For final production, chair blanks are first sheared to width from larger sheets of steel. Then holes are punched for the front-foot strip; edges and corners are rounded, and the blank is bent at five points.

4. One version is powder-coated red, blue, black, or gray. Another version (not shown) is in stainless steel that has been grain-sanded and finished with a clear powder coating. Highlighted by the blue circle, the front-foot strip is black acetate on the painted version and poly-carbonate on the stainless-steel version.

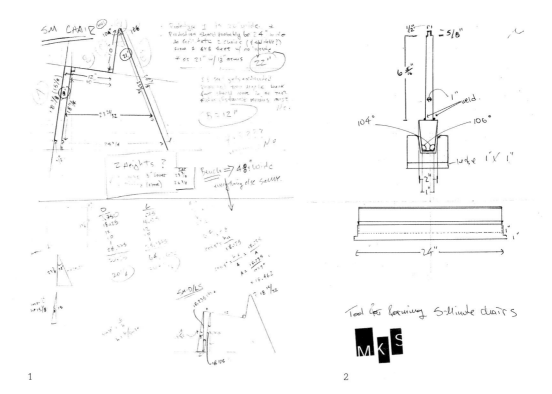

1

2

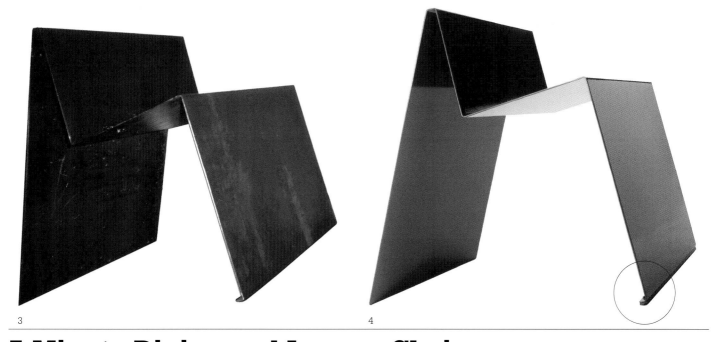

3

4

5-Minute Dining and Lounge Chairs

Designer	Adam Simha (American, b. 1966)
Manufacturer	MKS Design, Cambridge, Massachusetts, US
Date of design	2002
Materials	Mild steel and acetal; or stainless steel and polycarbonate
Size (mm/in.)	Side chair: 533/21 wide, 686/27 high, 686/27 deep at bottom; lounge chair: 533/21 wide, 584/23 high, 686/27 deep at bottom

Simha was reared in Cambridge, home of the Massachusetts Institute of Technology, where his father was the director of planning for 40 years. He admits to his good fortune in being frequently exposed to the sagacity of some of the architects and designers in the community. He eventually studied physics at MIT, made ice-cream and cooked professionally, and, for a time, studied percussion performance at the Berklee College of Music in Boston, but left due to a hand injury. While continuing culinary and other activities, he recalls: "I began metalwork in 1995 on a whim with a welding class and was hooked

immediately. And soon it became clear that, at long last, I'd found what I needed." Three years later he founded MKS Design, named for his wife's initials, and devoted himself full time to the enterprise five years ago.

In a quest for "a free and unselfconscious mix of fact, function, wit, and whimsy," Simha proposes: "The design of a chair should address the reality of the experience of sitting: inherently one of changing needs and desires."

The name 5-Minute came from the time taken to make the first prototype. Production of the final design was more complicated than its appearance might suggest.

1

2

1–2. Ergonomic studies were conducted for incline angle and contour.

3. A prototype was developed.

4. An isometric drawing provided information on precise form, curves, angles, etc.

5. Polyurethane is injection-molded in one piece within male and female dies. The mold is shown open.

The matte finish is photo-engraved and scratch-resistant. The spherical, nongrooved texture resists dirt accumulation.

3

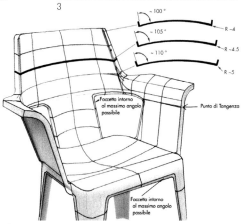

4

5

Altra-Ergo Stacking Outdoor Side Chair

Designer	Peter Solomon (American, b. 1965)
Manufacturer	Altra Design Limited, London, UK
Date of design	2002
Materials	Polypropylene
Size (mm/in.)	640/25⅛ wide, 820/32¼ high, 580/22¹³⁄₁₆ deep

Solomon, who studied industrial design at the Pratt Institute in New York, has been a professional designer for 19 years. He lived in Los Angeles for a time before attending the Domus Academy in Milan, Italy, where his studio is now located. Commissions have ranged from mobile phones and sports equipment to train interiors and furniture, such as the Altra-Ergo Stacking Chair.

A recipient of the prestigious Compasso d'Oro award, he reveals that he has "a passion for Italian design" which he combines with "the practicality of American technology."

His stacking chair, announced as a new concept in

outdoor seating, is comfortable and durable, serves ecological and ergonomic concerns, and seeks a wide public. The manufacturer rhetorically inquires: "Why not realize design objects to be sold at low prices in large do-it-yourself stores?"—answering: "This was the challenge Peter Solomon posed to himself some years ago, which became the inspiration for his collaboration with [us]."

The firm's cofounder, John Caulkins, explains: "Our objective is to prove that anyone can afford to buy a design object like the Altra-Ergo Chair and be proud to have it in their home."

1

2

3

1. The designer/maker welds in his New England workshop.

2. The diameter of today's American quarter, or 25-cent coin, is 24 mm/$^{15}/_{16}$ in.

3. Coins are adhered with a "U"-shaped metal wire that is welded at the back-side edges of the coins. The coins are not welded edge-to-edge so as to eliminate the appearance of the welding solder on the surface.

4. Also welded, the support structure and legs are stainless steel.

4

Quarter Side Chair

Designer	Johnny Swing (American, b. 1961)
Manufacturer	Johnny Swing Welding Co., Brookline, Vermont, US
Date of design	2002
Materials	US-minted 25-cent coins and stainless steel
Size (mm/in.)	480/19 wide, 965/38 high, 508/20 deep

Johnny Swing, a pseudonym, studied at Skidmore College and the Skowhegan School of Painting and Sculpture in the US and has been a professional artist for the last two decades—primarily in New York's Greenwich Village and now in New England.

He has created furniture and interiors for corporate clients. Eventually he achieved some fame by serving as the team leader on the American television series "Junkyard Wars," in which garbage is picked through to provide waste to recycle into new products.

Similarly, Swing's furniture gives new life to ordinary

objects—such as the Quarter Chair, the fourth in his Obsessive Furniture Line series. His original intention was to make a simple, cost-effective chair. However, according to Swing: "This goal failed, and my more artistic obligations seemed to have resurfaced into sensual shapes held together by intricate, architectural structures. With this as my true goal, I think that the Quarter Chair is one of my sexiest."

In an April 26, 2004, interview in *Provincetown Magazine*, a local periodical published on Cape Cod, Massachusetts, he is quoted as saying: "I used to care

what people would think about sitting in one of my pieces. I'd want to know. Now, it's more like whether they can meet the challenge, sitting in something I've designed.

"I want to make new shapes. [And] yes, there are new shapes to be made. But that's what someone with an ego would say. I mean, there's only so much you can do with furniture. We still have backs, asses, legs that continue to do the same they've always done. That's not about to change. But I think I can [do something new]."

Aside from its use of coins, the Quarter Chair is greatly enhanced by its solution for connecting coin to coin.

1

2

1–2. A small but powerful Gearmotion servomotor (1) is inserted into the bottom-front stainless-steel tube (2, see the red circle). This type of battery-operated DC motor (120 volts, 6 rpm) has a drive shaft that turns when a code signals the Elenco AK-510 motion detector (also inset into a tube), available to the designer in kit form. The detector is pyroelectric-infrared (PIR) sensitive. In this case, when someone nears the chair in its erect position, it lowers to the flat-seat position. And rises again when the sitter departs. This type of infrared motion-detector is also used for alarm systems and public-toilet flushers.

3–6. Sequential images illustrate the descent.

3

4

5

6

Ooga-Ooga Side Chair

Designer	Ezri Tarazi (Israeli, b. 1962)
Manufacturer	Prototype
Date of design	2004
Materials	Steel tubing, Gearmotion servomotor, pyroelectric-infrared (PIR) sensor
Size (mm/in.)	Flat-up position: 472/18⁹⁄₁₆ wide, 1350/53⅛ high, 450/17¾ deep; full-down position: 480/18⅞ wide, 940/37 high, 480/18⅞ deep

Tarazi is professor in the industrial-design department of the Bezalel Academy in Jerusalem, where he also studied. He has worked for a number of firms, been a partner of IDEO Israel, and a freelance designer.

His large quantity and wide range of work has included high-tech products as well as unusual low-tech items that have called on readymades—or preexisting objects—such as building a chair from rolled newspapers.

His Ooga-Ooga Chair is an example of the former. Activated by a motion-detector, the chair lowers or rises when someone comes near or, after sitting on it, walks away.

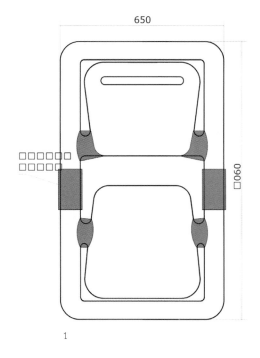

2

1. A one-piece form is computer-numeric-cut from a three-poured-layer PMMA plastic sheet (15 mm/⅝ in. thick). The red areas in the drawing indicate where hot blades are applied to make the plastic pliable for bending.

2. The sheet, while hot in the six areas to be bent, is then placed over the

mold and pressed into place. The mold is built of plywood.

3. A version of the chair features one-color PMMA. (The black version is not shown.) A table is made in the same manner as the chair.

4. The chair, for indoor or outdoor use, is stackable.

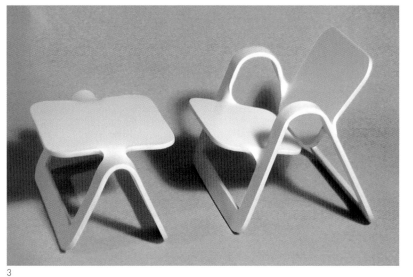

3

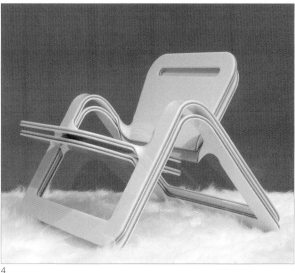

4

Slice Stacking Lounge Chair

Designer	Alexis Tricoire (France, b. 1967)
Manufacturer	AG Products, Aytré, France
Date of design	2004
Materials	Polymethyl methacrylate (PMMA)
Size (mm/in.)	640/25³⁄₁₆ wide, 550/21⅝ high, 700/27⁹⁄₁₆ deep

Tricoire established his own studio about a decade ago after studying at the École Nationale Supérieure des Arts Décoratifs and the ENSAAMA and working with architect Sylvain Dubuisson, designer Pucci de Rossi, and others, all in Paris, his birthplace. He also attended the School of the Art Institute of Chicago.

Should the simple production methods behind his Slice Chair not be known, it might look as though it had been created by more sophisticated technology. And the use of a single material—a sandwich of three poured layers of PMMA—optimizes recycling.

1. The idea of a chair whose seat is separate from the back traveled through a number of possible solutions.

2–5. Computer renderings explored the back/seat disconnection.

6. Only four elements—back, seat, carpet, and floor flange—and four bolts compose the configuration.

1

2

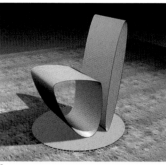

3

4

5

6

'Til We Meet Side Chair

Designers	Umamy (Eran Apelbaum, b. 1964; Sarit Atziz, b. 1969; Doron Oryan, b. 1969; and Yohanan Siskindovich, b. 1970), Israeli
Manufacturer	Umamy, Tel Aviv, Israel
Date of design	2002
Materials	Steel, leather, textiles
Size (mm/in.)	Chair: 420/16⁹⁄₁₆ wide, 760/29¹⁵⁄₁₆ high, 420/16⁹⁄₁₆ deep; carpet: 1200/47¼ dia.

A group of designers founded Umamy in Tel Aviv seven years ago to "pose probing existential questions."

'Til We Meet Again typifies their widely published, unusual, and provocative body of work. The chair, the designers explain, "asks consumers whether the general assumption that a seat and a back be firmly attached is valid. Although physically comfortable, this chair plays havoc with our expectations and sense of security."

After an initial reaction of surprise, the user might say: "Oh, now I understand its secret." Even so, 'Til We Meet Again remains visually intriguing.

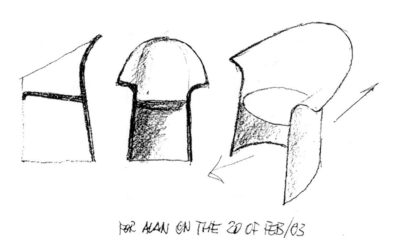

1. A sketch by Massimo Vignelli is labeled "FOR ALAN [HELLER] ON THE 20TH OF FEB/03."

2. A somewhat more formal Vignelli sketch provides dimensions. Only the seat height was retained for the final model.

3. A computer rendering, possibly in CAD format.

Due to the floating appearance of the seat, the chair seems to be of two separate, fused elements. It is actually one piece, formed by the rotational molding of a polymeric resin. Both the one-side die (no male and female sections) and the one-piece formation appreciably lessen production costs.

1

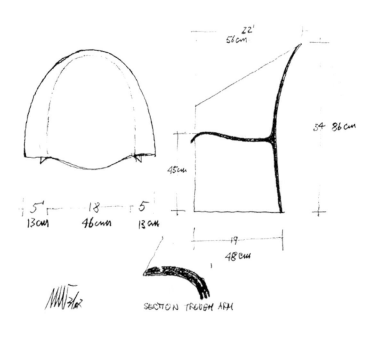

2

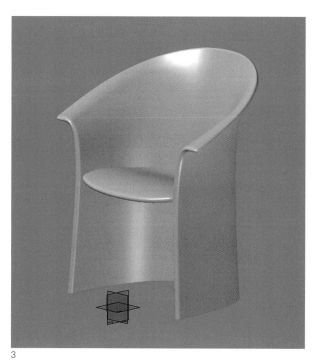

3

The Vignelli Chair

Designers	Lella Vignelli (Italian, b. 1934) and Massimo Vignelli (Italian, b. 1931)
Manufacturer	Heller Incorporated, New York, New York, US
Date of design	2003
Materials	Polymer
Size (mm/in.)	780/30¹¹⁄₁₆ wide, 900/35⁷⁄₁₆ high, 565/22¼ deep, 440/17⁵⁄₁₆ seat height

Alan Heller's eponymous New York firm was established to make well-designed, reasonably priced items for the home. The first of its products was the 1970 Max 2 Stacking Cups by Massimo Vignelli. At about this time, Vignelli and his wife, Lella, set up a studio in New York. Since then the couple have designed a vast number of products, interiors, and graphics, some with others, including four studio associates.

Over a quarter of a century later, again for Heller, the Vignellis have designed a chair, true to their principles of simplicity, roto-molded as one piece.

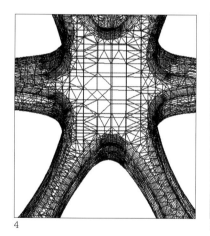

1. An exploded drawing of the six parts—back, seat, and four legs. The chair could not be made in one piece due to the size of the building room of the sintering machine. The machine used costs 500,000 euros.

2–3. The designers offer these drawings as examples of the inspiration of coral formations. The drawing are by Ernst Haeckel (1834–1919), the renowned German comparative anatomist.

4–6. Computer drawings (close-up and full views) show wire structures that indicate the static lines (much like Haeckel's coral drawings) of the basic framework of the chair.

The designers developed a questionnaire on which a customer would state his or her preferences concerning favorite music, authors, movies, etc. The data is matched to the basic structure of a chair which can be produced within a few hours.

The process of selective laser sintering (SLS®) by machinery, in this case, by the 3D-Systems firm:

The single material is a plastic powder that can be nylon, glass-filled nylon, rubberlike DSM Somos® resin, Truform, or Duraform polyamide nylon. The material for the Sinterchair® is nylon.

Nylon powder is applied in fine layers.

A computer-instructed laser traces an outline (or two-dimensional segment of the shape) into the powder.

A shape is cut out, layer by layer. And each layer hardens.

Ultimately, a three-dimensional form is formed from a block of closely packed and fused white powder.

When fully formed, the shape is removed from the block.

1

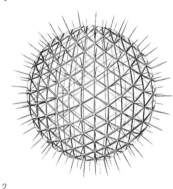

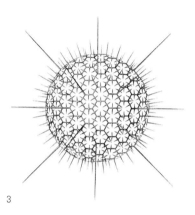

2   3

4   5   6

Sinterchair®

Designers	Oliver Vogt (German, b. 1966) and Hermann Weizenegger (German, b. 1963)
Manufacturer	A demonstration example
Date of design	2002
Materials	Nylon powder
Size (mm/in.)	Variable

Oliver Vogt and Hermann Weizenegger have become well known for their idea of using blind artisans and others at Berlin's Blindenanstalt to build products by accomplished professional designers. (See pp. 30–31.)

While the pair have designed a number of products for firms—from Authentics to Thomas/Rosenthal—the Sinterchair® is an imaginative self-assignment to make furniture that is specifically configured to an individual consumer's personality and that can be produced very quickly.

Describing the project, they present the following justification: "Just imagine buying your furniture like made-

to-measure suits…. You walk into a shop; tell the assistant what you are looking for; have him draw out something corresponding to your individual wishes on his computer, and he manufactures it for you on the spot. You receive a one-off product, tailored to your personal taste and your requirements, that is ready for you to take home with you within 24 hours."

The new production technique that makes this possible is a sintering machine—selective laser sintering (SLS®)—of the type currently employed for model-making in design studios.

Desiring to produce "the chair of the future," the designers ask: "But why a chair? [Because] a chair is *the* object of design, not only for us. A chair design always illustrates the current status of society and its technological achievements [by combining] know-how with materials and aesthetic sentiments to form a seating sculpture linked to man's cultural history like no other item might." As examples, they point to Thonet's No. 14 Chair of 1859–60, the 1920s tubular-steel furniture of the Bauhaus era, and Verner Panton's 1959–60 one-piece-plastic S Chair. For its time, the Sinterchair® is also cutting edge.

1. The components:
   Four rolls of dense wool felt (8 mm/¼ in. thick) for the outside layers;
   Two rolls of soft wool felt (25 mm/1 in. thick) for the inside layers;
   Three M8 threaded metal rods;
   Six custom-made stainless-steel caps to screw onto each end of the rods.

2. Holes are stamped into the felt. The rods are fed through the holes.

3. A partially assembled chair, here in one color but possible in others (see the facing page).

1

2

3

Joseph Felt Chair

Designer	Lothar Windels (German, b. 1967)
Manufacturer	Parentesi Quadra by Extrabilia S.r.l., Quarrata (PT), Italy
Date of design	2000
Materials	Wool felt, M8 metal rods, stainless-steel caps
Size (mm/in.)	1100/43⁵⁄₁₆ wide, 800/31½ high, 900/35⁷⁄₁₆ deep

Windels, who studied at the Technische Hochschule in Darmstadt, Rhode Island School of Design, and London's Royal College of Art, teaches at the Rhode Island School.

The lounge chair is named for Windels's fellow German, the artist Joseph Beuys, known for his predilection for felt.

The chair is made up entirely of felt, held together by only three rods.

The shape will alter through use. Windels compares it to "a leather shoe that is broken in over time. Its form changes according to its main user. The chair gets personalized through wear."

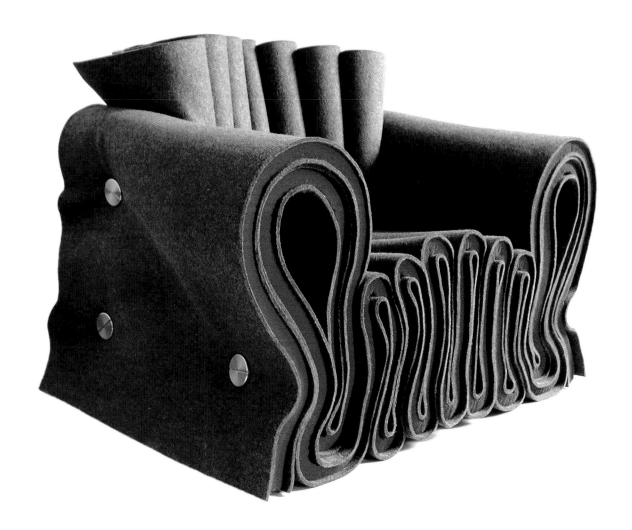